Free Sports Memorabilia

Where to Get It

Free
Sports
Memorabilia
Where to Get It

Elizabeth B. Fulgaro
& John M. Fulgaro

BETTERWAY PUBLICATIONS, INC.
WHITE HALL, VIRGINIA

Published by Betterway Publications, Inc.
P.O. Box 219
Crozet, VA 22932
(904) 823-5661

Cover design and photograph by Susan Riley
Photographs by Elizabeth and John Fulgaro
Typography by East Coast Typography, Inc.

Fulgaro, Elizabeth B.
    Free sports memorabilia : where to get it / Elizabeth B. Fulgaro,
John M. Fulgaro.
        p.   cm.
    Includes index.
    Summary: Presents a variety of methods of collecting sports
-related memorabilia at little or no cost.
    ISBN 1-55870-181-8
    1. Sports—Collectibles—Juvenile literature.   2. Free material-
—Juvenile literature. [1. Sports—Collectibles.   2. Free
material.] I. Fulgaro, John M., 1956- . II. Title.
GV568.5.F85 1991
796′.075—dc20   90-21716
                                                   CIP
                                                   AC

Printed in the United States of America
0 9 8 7 6 5 4 3 2 1

To Grandmother, Maxine McSweeny Hjelte, who pioneered it all.

Contents

INTRODUCTION

How to Use this Book

Collection of sports-related memorabilia does not have to be an expensive hobby. The purpose of *Free Sports Memorabilia* is to present a variety of alternative methods to collect sports-related memorabilia at little or no cost.

The book was written for both novice and veteran collectors. Those new to the hobby will be introduced to over 50 ways to collect sports-related memorabilia on a limited budget. For veterans, *Free Sports Memorabilia* is more than a simple refresher course on familiar techniques. The book actually increases the veteran's potential return from collecting techniques by covering novel approaches to the hobby, as well as traditional methods.

Free Sports Memorabilia features over fifty techniques, each detailed with step-by-step instructions, to help you put together a large collection of the memorabilia you want, given limited time and a small budget. It is designed to help you maximize your collecting efforts by saving you time, money, and frustration. Complete with sample letters and useful addresses to complement the collecting techniques, *Free Sports Memorabilia* supplies everything you need to spend less time figuring out what to do and more time enjoying your collection.

Unlike many self-help books, you don't need to read *Free Sports Memorabilia* cover to cover to benefit from it. Each section of the book can be used by itself or together with the other sections. In this way, you read and use only what interests you and avoid wasting valuable time on the rest.

The book is divided into three major areas:
Collectors' Tools
Collectors' Techniques
Collectors' Resources

Collectors' Tools

If you truly want to get the most — both emotionally and financially — from the time you spend collecting, you need to spend some up-front time identifying what you hope to gain from the hobby and what tools are at your disposal to accomplish this. *Collectors' Tools* encourages you to set up and maintain a solid foundation for your collection, then details how to go about it. Sample worksheets are included to minimize the effort you will need to make.

Collectors' Techniques

Using the Table of Contents, you quickly can identify and refer to the individual collection techniques most interesting to you. Each technique featured begins with a brief summary of the idea behind the technique and what return you can expect. The summary is followed by step-by-step instructions for using the technique. Frequently, where written correspondence is suggested, generic sample letters are supplied. You can quickly customize these for your own needs.

Collectors' Resources

The Collectors' Resources portion of the book consists of an extensive series of Appendices that list various addresses and other references to ease your pursuit of free and low cost sports-related memorabilia. These include information such as: recent addresses for all major league baseball, basketball, football, and hockey teams; recent addresses for corporations known to have previously sponsored sports-related promotions; lists of sports-related periodicals; etc. Throughout the Collectors' Techniques section, you are referred to the appropriate appendix in Collectors' Resources that will make execution of the technique easy. The Collectors' Resources section also can be used alone to assist you in pursuit of your own proprietary collection techniques that may not be covered in the book.

Free Sports Memorabilia was created to save you time and money and maximize the enjoyment, as well as the results, you gain from your collection of free and low cost sports-related

INTRODUCTION (continued)

memorabilia. Have fun with the various techniques and resources at your disposal in this book. As you experiment with them, you will find that at any given moment a technique may produce surprisingly effective or shockingly disappointing results, depending on the responsiveness of the person or people you approach. But over time, using *Free Sports Memorabilia* should increase the personal pleasure you get from your hobby at the very least. Who knows, potentially the financial profit will increase as well.

HAPPY COLLECTING!

Part I
Collectors' Tools

The Want List
Collection Inventory
Valuing Your Collection

THE WANT LIST

In pursuit of great ideas sometimes there is a tendency to overlook the obvious. For this reason *Free Sports Memorabilia* begins with a reminder of one of the most useful tools for collecting the memorabilia you desire.

MAINTAIN AN UP-TO-DATE WANT LIST!

Every collector should maintain an up-to-date list of those items you want in your collection. The want list can be as simple as a random itemization of memorabilia you wish were in your collection and can be written on a scratch piece of paper. Or it can be a detailed list of items targeted for your collection, including information such as acquisition priorities — which items you would like first, notes regarding potential acquisition strategies and sources, and progress to date.

Whether a casual or serious collector, the value of a want list to your hobby cannot be over-emphasized. It serves a myriad of purposes.

Obviously, the more detailed your want list is, the more quickly and profitably you will be able to react to unexpected collecting opportunities. But on a more basic level, the want list gives a focus to your collecting activities. Whether intentional or not, establishing and maintaining your want list forces you to set goals and priorities for your collection. With want list in hand, when opportunity presents itself, you immediately will know whether or not to capitalize on it. This is because, to put it bluntly, you will know what you want, and just as important, what you don't want! In a world with seemingly unlimited collecting options, your want list is like an insurance policy guaranteeing that the time you have for the hobby is spent in pursuit of those items that would mean the most to you. Besides, without focus you could spend all that valuable hobby time and lose limited storage space to gain memorabilia of little or no long-term meaning to you.

It may seem difficult to develop a want list, especially if you've never collected before. You may not even know what different types of memorabilia are available, let alone what you want to collect. Appendix V in the Collectors' Resource section gives you a partial list of the types of memorabilia available for collecting. But the place to begin your want list is with yourself.

Collecting is a very personal, individualized process. Memorabilia that brings you enjoyment won't necessarily be the same as the memorabilia that brings enjoyment to other collectors. And the purpose of a hobby, most experts will agree, is personal satisfaction, *not* monetary reward. Should monetary reward happen to coincide with personal pleasure, so much the better. But profit should not be your primary motivation to pursue collecting low cost sports-related memorabilia, for you could be sorely disappointed. Escalating values of all sports-related memorabilia are in no way assured.

Your want list, especially for free memorabilia, should be made up of items of interest to you, whether or not others would give it the same value. If you're unsure how to begin your want list, start by asking yourself why you initially became interested in collecting sports-related memorabilia. Did it begin with the idea of accumulating everything associated with one particular sport, team, or player? Or perhaps a certain type of memorabilia, such as autographs or game schedules, regardless of sport, perked your interest. One positive aspect of collecting is that there is no *wrong* way. So whatever sparked your interest, that is the direction in which to start. As you learn more about what's available and what brings you the most satisfaction, you can update your want list, thereby giving your collecting efforts even more focus with hopefully increasing results.

An updated want list does help you maximize opportunities to collect the sports-related memorabilia you seek. To make the most of your want list (and ultimately your collection), keep a copy of your updated want list with you at all times. You never know when the opportunity will arise to use it. You'll know exactly what gifts to request for birthdays and holidays. If the topic comes up with friends, you can mention you are a collector. Should they show a mutual interest, you can refer to your list to see if there is any potential for trades. When you visit trade shows, in addition to checking out the vendor booths you might strike up conver-

THE WANT LIST (continued)

sations with other attendees. If your want list is handy and an opportunity to trade arises, you'll know exactly what to ask for and maybe even what you would be willing to give up in return.

COLLECTION INVENTORY

Half the fun of collecting is being able to review, show, and tell about what you have. Next to your want list (and a copy of this book), the most useful tool to maximizing your collection is to maintain an up-to-date inventory of your sports-related memorabilia.

An up-to-date inventory gives you a quick overview of your collection so you can keep track of how your collection is progressing. You can easily see if your collection activities are producing the results you had planned. At a glance, your inventory reminds you of items already acquired. Simultaneously, it highlights targeted parts of your collection that are still incomplete, assisting you in the maintenance of a productive want list. In addition, your inventory can expose items that no longer serve a purpose in your current collection. Once identified, these items can be used in trading or selling opportunities. Without an up-to-date inventory, they might have remained forgotten excesses in your collection rather than effective tools to help you further your collection efforts. Depending on the detail included in your inventory, it can even indicate the quality of your memorabilia, helping you target areas where you want to upgrade the quality of your collection.

Just as with your want list, your collection inventory can be as simple or complex as you choose. It may just be jotted down randomly on a scrap of paper or be an organized, in-depth listing such as could be done using the Inventory Sheets found in the last section of this book. As such, it could include information such as an item's date and place of acquisition, its condition, and recent indications of its potential resale value.

Your inventory is important in keeping an overview of your growing collection. Its existence eliminates the need to rely on memory, freeing your brain for more productive tasks and reducing the potential for duplication of efforts.

If you are just beginning to collect, it is easy to start your inventory log at the same time. Make a note of each addition to your collection as it occurs. Veteran collectors who have never kept track of their collection's inventory face

Inventories can be organized by type of memorabilia, such as stickers and decals.

COLLECTION INVENTORY (continued)

the more tedious task of inventorying what they already have. It may seem a too cumbersome task to undertake, but it is well worth the effort. And once you've completed your first inventory register, it is easy to maintain.

The best method for managing your collection's inventory is likely to be unique to you, since each collector has different goals. Depending on the focus of your collection, the organization of your inventory will vary. For example, if your focus were the autographs of major league baseball players, you might organize your inventory alphabetically by player name. On the other hand, if you collected all memorabilia related to a particular NFL team you might inventory it by type of memorabilia. In Appendix Z of the Collectors' Resources section several sample inventory sheets are included, which illustrate alternative ways to inventory your collection. These sheets serve as a starting point. If you don't have an inventory system in place for your collection already, use these examples as a starting point to customize an inventory register to suit your collection's unique needs.

As your collection grows, you might also feel a need to have it insured against damage, theft, or loss. Your inventory serves as the foundation for presenting the information your insurance professional needs to make certain your policy gives you proper coverage. It is a good idea to keep a copy of your most recently updated inventory register in a fire-proof location at all times.

Your goal is to have a method of inventorying your collection that gives you the most productive way to quickly overview information regarding your collection. Your inventory allows you to see where your collection has been and where it is headed. Its role is important to getting the most from your collection efforts.

VALUING YOUR COLLECTION

Ideally, your collection will not only bring you enjoyment, but could prove to be an appreciating financial asset as well. Primarily, you are encouraged to collect because of the enjoyment your collection brings you. Whether the activity of collecting provides a pleasant pastime or the items in your collection bring happy memories to mind, this should be your primary motivation for collecting, not making a fortune.

However, this does not mean you should completely ignore the potential resale value of your memorabilia, as well as memorabilia targeted for future collection. As far as it is possible, it is important to have an idea of the value of the sports-related memorabilia that interests you. This knowledge will give you negotiation power to take advantage of acquisition and trading opportunities that present themselves, and in a manner that is productive for all involved. In addition, as your collection grows you will need to have an assessment of your collection's value should you desire an insurance policy that would compensate you for any lost, stolen, or damaged items.

There are many sources that claim to assist collectors in valuing their memorabilia. The most common sources typically restrict their valuations almost exclusively to sports trading cards. A list of some of these can be found in Appendix W under the Collectors' Resources section.

It may prove more difficult to establish values for less common types of memorabilia. Dealers could be a good source. You can obtain appraisals by visiting dealer retail establishments, corresponding with mail order dealers, or talking with dealers represented at trade shows. Of course, what dealers would pay you for your memorabilia is likely to be substantially less than what it could be resold for to their retail customers. The difference, after all, represents the dealer's profit.

More obscure memorabilia might be a candidate for valuation by an experienced auctioneer who knows what bids such items have brought. Usually an auctioneer will charge a fee for his or her appraisal services. You must decide if the fee represents a worthwhile investment of your funds.

VALUING YOUR COLLECTION (continued)

You can privately keep informal track of the changing values of sports-related memorabilia by reading periodicals that cater specifically to sports memorabilia collectors. You will find several of these referenced in Appendix W. Sometimes you can read back issues at your local libraries. Other times you must decide if the price of the subscription is worth paying, given your particular needs.

Ultimately, your collection is only worth as much as someone is willing to pay for it at any given moment. Don't invest too much time attempting to put a value on your collection, but keep your eyes and ears open to price trends in general within the hobby.

Keep tabs on what others are selling and at what price. You may be surprised to see what your collectibles are worth.

Part II
Collectors' Techniques

Sport-Direct
Autographs
Trades
Media
Retail Promotions
Public Sale
Civic

LEAGUE OFFICES

Getting Started

It's amazing what you can get when you ask. The League Offices exist not only to manage, but also to market and promote the leagues' teams. Contact league office headquarters with an information request and frequently you'll receive free memorabilia in return. During 1989, in response to a telephone inquiry, the NFL sent a beautiful color booklet with information regarding all NFL teams and their stadiums.

Even if your inquiry doesn't result in direct memorabilia, the information they send will most likely give you some new potential memorabilia sources you hadn't otherwise considered.

Steps

☐ Refer to Appendix Q for the addresses and phone numbers of league office headquarters for Baseball, Basketball, Football, and Hockey Leagues.

☐ You can write, but it is easier to call league offices for information. Even if the call is long distance, you won't be on the phone long. Ask the Public Relations Department to send you any information regarding their league available for fans.

☐ Be aware of bad times to call. Often entire public relations departments are out of their offices and at the games during playoffs and championships.

INDIVIDUAL TEAM PROMOTIONS

Getting Started

Contact your targeted sports teams directly and let them know you are a fan who collects team-, sport-, or player-related memorabilia. You never know what you will receive. Some teams send a plethora of items such as schedules, stickers, newsletters, etc. Other teams may ignore your request completely. For the price of a postage stamp, it's worth a try.

Steps

☐ See Appendices in the Collectors' Resources section for the addresses of all professional baseball, basketball, football, and hockey teams.

☐ Using a letter such as the following, write those teams that interest you.

✉

Team Name
Team Address

Attn: Public Relations Department

Dear Team Public Relations Department,

I am a longtime, loyal fan of (insert name of team here). I also collect team-related memorabilia. Please send me any material on the team you feel would be of interest to me.

A self-addressed, stamped envelope is enclosed for your response. Thank you for your attention to my request. I look forward to hearing from you soon.

Signed,

Your Name
Your Address

✉

☐ Always enclose a large self-addressed, stamped envelope to make it convenient for them to respond to your request.

TEAM PUBLIC RELATIONS DEPARTMENTS

Getting Started

Every team in every sport wants a positive public image. To help ensure they achieve this objective most have public relations departments to convey their desired image to the public.

Team Public Relations Departments can be a source of special team-related information, such as the media kits most put together annually. These are given to print, radio, and TV journalists and present the teams in a favorable light. These media kits are usually available for a small fee. You can either make the decision to pay their price, or you could write them and ask whether leftover kits are available after the season at a reduced cost.

Steps

☐ Refer to the Appendices in the Collectors' Resources section for the addresses of the teams you wish to contact.

☐ Contact the teams by telephone or by a letter such as the one below, inquiring about the availability of low cost, or no cost, media kits.

Stickers, photos, decals, wristbands, pencils, and more; these are all for the price of a first class postage stamp. Team Public Relations Departments love to hear from fans.

TEAM PUBLIC RELATIONS DEPARTMENTS (continued)

✉

Team Name
Team Address

Attn: Public Relations Department

Dear Team Public Relations Department,

I am a longtime fan of (insert name of team here) and an avid collector of team-related sports memorabilia. I am especially interested in media kits featuring team information, which you might make available.

Are these media kits made available to fans such as myself? If so, is there a cost involved?

Due to the limited funds I have available for my memorabilia collection, I would be interested in learning what happens to outdated media kits leftover at the end of a given season. Are they currently, or could they be, made available for no or low cost?

Enclosed is a stamped, self-addressed envelope for your response. I would be happy to supply as well the envelope with correct postage for you to forward media kits, once they are available.

Thank you for your attention to my questions. I look forward to hearing from you soon.

Signed,

Your Name
Your Address

✉

GAME PROMOTIONS

Getting Started

Do what you like best. Attend sporting events and obtain free sports memorabilia. To increase attendance, most sports teams give away promotional items during the year. This is a great opportunity to obtain free merchandise, especially if your collection emphasizes memorabilia from your local team.

Steps

☐ Refer to the Appendices in the Collectors' Resources section for a complete list of major league baseball, hockey, basketball, and football team addresses.

☐ Send a letter such as this sample to the public relations department of the teams in which you are interested.

✉

Team Name
Team Address

Attn: Public Relations Department

Dear Public Relations Representative,

I am a great fan of (insert name of team here) and enjoy attending games. I would appreciate a list of all promotions scheduled for games this year.

A self-addressed, stamped envelope is enclosed for your convenience. Thank for your prompt attention to this request.

Signed,

Your Name
Your Address

✉

Season schedules provide you with the dates of special fan appreciation and give-away nights, and are also a unique, beautiful, but lesser-known collectible.

GAME PROMOTIONS
(continued)

☐ In return for your letters, you will usually receive a list similar to the following 1989 sample:

TORONTO BLUE JAYS

April 14:	Calendar Day
April 15:	Poster Day
April 23:	Watch Day
May 7:	Bat Day
May 22:	Thermal Bag Day
May 27:	Sports Bag Day
June 17:	Visor Day
June 18:	Seat Cushion Day
July 1:	Travel Mug Day
July 16:	Cap Day
Aug. 26:	Old Timers Game
Aug. 27:	Wallet Day
Sept. 3:	Autographed Ball Day

☐ Use the calendar to determine what games to attend to receive the merchandise that interests you most. If you cannot attend, find a non-collecting friend who is going and is willing to pick up the "freebie" for you.

☐ Another source for calendars of game "freebie" promotions are periodicals geared to collectors of sports-related memorabilia (listing of several available in Appendix W). In the interest of their readers often they will include these schedules for the various teams at the beginning of the season.

☐ Check to see if your public library subscribes to the periodicals. If so, you can get the information at no cost. If not, you must decide if the cost of the subscription is warranted, given the information you seek.

☐ Don't forget about minor league and senior league teams. To promote attendance they often give away potential future memorabilia as well. Use the same technique of writing the teams directly to screen which games to attend to maximize your collection.

GAME PROGRAMS/ SCORECARDS

Getting Started

Collect a multitude of game programs from most sports without spending a dime. When everyone else jams the aisles to leave the sports complex as soon as the event is over, take a deep breath, relax, and stay in your seat. Then take a few minutes and survey your general area. Many people discard their programs and score-cards immediately and leave them on their seats after the game. Pick up the ones that are in the best condition and your mission is accomplished.

In addition, you will want to contact the team directly (see information on all major league baseball, basketball, football, and ice hockey teams in the Appendices) after games regarding extra programs they printed, but were unable to sell. Sometimes you can pick these up at substantial discounts to game-time prices.

Steps

☐ Attend games! When you are unable to attend, check with a friend who is and see if they are willing to take a few minutes to pick up discarded programs and scorecards after the game for you.

☐ Take a minute to relax after the game ends and pick up programs and scorecards other fans have left behind. Not only will your collection benefit, but your stress level will as well. Eliminate being squished in the crowd. Let others fight the losing battle of beating fellow fans out of the parking lot.

☐ Telephone teams after games to ask about programs that went unsold. Should you decide to acquire some, make sure you send a self-addressed, stamped envelope to make it easy for the team to send you the merchandise.

Frequently other fans discard their programs, which you can collect for free when the game is over.

Fan clubs are a good way to get memorabilia and information on teams or individual players.

FAN CLUBS

Getting Started

Although membership in a team fan club may involve a small up-front cost, it provides a wide variety of opportunities to acquire unique sports memorabilia, frequently for lower cost than through dealers or retail outlets. For instance, sometimes unique memorabilia is made available exclusively to members of fan clubs. In addition, the fan club's membership roster provides a valuable resource of other potential memorabilia collectors with whom you might be able to establish productive trading relationships.

Steps

☐ Look up the addresses of the professional baseball, basketball, football, or ice hockey teams that interest you in the Appendices of the Collectors' Resources Section.

☐ Send a letter such as the following asking for a list of fan clubs:

Team Name
Team Address

Attn: Public Relations Department

Dear Public Relations Department,

    I am a longtime loyal fan of (insert name of team here). I am interested in possibly joining a team fan club. Please send me a list of the various fan clubs that exist. Telephone numbers of persons to contact as well as addresses would be helpful.

    Any information you can provide would be appreciated. A self-addressed, stamped envelope is provided for your response. I look forward to hearing from you soon.

Signed,

Your Name
Your Address

FAN CLUBS (continued)

☐ Research by telephone or mail the benefits and services available fan clubs offer members. A letter such as the following may prove helpful:

✉

Contact Person's Name
Fan Club Name
Fan Club Address

Dear (insert name of contact person here),

I am a longtime, loyal fan of (insert name of professional sports team here). I am interested in finding out about your fan club.

Please send any information you have regarding how your fan club works, the services members can expect, cost to join, etc.

I am also an avid collector of team-related memorabilia. Please tell me how membership in your club might help me improve my collection. Is your membership roster available to fellow members? I would be interested in contacting others who might share my interest if I joined the club. Do you have a membership periodical or newsletter where I might make other members aware of my willingness to trade with other collectors?

Thank you for your assistance. A self-addressed, stamped envelope is enclosed for your response. I look forward to hearing from you soon.

Signed,

Your Name
Your Address

✉

☐ Once you've received the information, weigh any cost against potential rewards.
☐ Should the benefits look worthwhile, join the fan club or clubs that you feel will benefit you and your collection most.

DISCARDED TEAM SUPPLIES/ EQUIPMENT

Getting Started

What happens to the team's cracked bats, worn practice balls, discarded mitts, and ripped uniforms? You'll never know unless you ask. Items that are considered worthless and would be discarded by a team or its suppliers could provide you with unique memorabilia that will enhance your own collection or can be used as bartering tools during future trading opportunities.

Steps

☐ Refer to the Appendices in the Collectors' Resources section to select the addresses of teams you propose to contact.
☐ Write the teams using a similar letter to find out whether you might acquire team supplies they plan to otherwise discard.

✉

Team Name
Team Address

Attn: Uniform and Equipment Supervisor

Dear Supervisor,

I am a longtime fan of (insert name of team here) and collect team-related memorabilia. Do you ever make discarded team equipment and uniforms available to fans such as myself? I would be happy to pay any shipping and handling costs.

I am interested in anything you might have to offer (or give a list of items you are especially interested in, i.e., bats, balls, uniforms, etc.). For your convenience I have enclosed a stamped, self-addressed envelope for your response. I look forward to hearing from you soon.

Signed,

Your Name
Your Address

DISCARDED TEAM SUPPLIES/ EQUIPMENT (continued)

☐ Write the teams of your choice, requesting the names of their suppliers.

✉

Team Name
Team Address

Attn: Team Uniform and Equipment Supervisor

Dear Supervisor,

I am a longtime fan of (insert name of team here) and collect team-related memorabilia.

If possible, please send me a list of those companies that supply your team with playing equipment and uniforms. I would like to contact them regarding the possibility of obtaining items produced but not purchased by the team, due to reasons such as poor quality, production overruns, or errors.

A self-addressed, stamped enveloped is enclosed for your response. Thank you for your assistance. I look forward to hearing from you soon.

Signed,

Your Name
Your Address

✉

DISCARDED TEAM SUPPLIES/ EQUIPMENT (continued)

☐ Should the team respond to your request, write the suppliers a letter.

✉

Supplier Company Name
Supplier Company Address

Attn: Customer Service Department

Dear Customer Service Department,

I am a longtime fan of (insert name of team here) and an avid collector of team-related sports memorabilia.

It is my understanding that you supply some of their team equipment and/or uniforms. Do you ever have merchandise remaining in your factory, which cannot be sold to the team because of production overruns, poor quality, player name misspellings, out-of-date styles, wrong sizes, etc.?

As a collector would there be any way for me to obtain some of this otherwise unsaleable merchandise? Please let me know if this is possible, what type of merchandise might be available, and what cost, if any, would be involved. A stamped, self-addressed envelope is enclosed for your convenience.

Thank you for your attention to my request. I look forward to hearing from you soon.

Signed,

Your Name
Your Address

✉

☐ It is most likely that suppliers will want to charge you for any merchandise, unless you represent a charitable cause and not your own collection.

☐ Negotiate in an attempt to arrive at a cost that is reasonable to the supplier and still fits your objectives of getting the memorabilia at a low cost.

PLAYER DISCARDED UNIFORMS/EQUIPMENT

Getting Started

Especially if you collect all memorabilia related to specific players, acquiring discarded playing uniforms and equipment used by these players could be a top priority of yours. Depending on how you handle your request, an individual player may respond to your wish to receive playing uniforms or equipment they are no longer using.

Of course, be sensitive to the fact that certain uniforms or pieces of equipment, though no longer in use, may have sentimental value to the player. Even to ask for items that obviously may have some sentimental attachment for the player is rude. For instance, you wouldn't want to ask a player for the jersey he wore in his World Series appearance, nor that from his first or last game.

Steps

☐ Refer to the Appendices in the Collectors' Resources section for a list of professional baseball, hockey, basketball, and football addresses.

☐ Select the addresses of those teams with players you wish to contact and send the players a letter such as this one.

PLAYER DISCARDED UNIFORMS/EQUIPMENT (continued)

Player Name
Team Name
Team Address

Dear Player Name,

I have been an avid fan of yours for a long time (or list an event you recall that really won your support as a fan). In fact, I even try to collect as much sports memorabilia about you as possible.

It would mean a great deal to me if you were willing to share with me one of your old, discarded uniforms, or a piece of playing equipment you no longer use. I would not want this to be an imposition and would be quite willing to pay for any shipping and handling costs.

For your convenience I have included a self-addressed, stamped envelope for your response. I look forward to hearing from you soon. Thank you for your time and attention to my request.

Signed,

Your Name
Your Address

✉

☐ Although your objective is to acquire free memorabilia, if the player you are contacting is a current star, he may be receiving many requests such as yours. To entice him to help you with your particular collection, you might offer to make a donation in his name to a charity of his choice in exchange for the memorabilia. Once again, you must decide if the cost would be justified by the reward. And don't even offer unless you are willing to follow through.

WOMEN'S SPORTS MEMORABILIA

Getting Started

Due to the fewer number of women playing sports professionally and the lack of media attention the existing professionals receive, there is understandably less sports-related memorabilia specifically related to women's sports. However, as women's sports gain in recognition and popularity the memorabilia should multiply. Whether over time women's and men's sports are combined or remain separate, this may be an opportunity to truly get in on the ground floor of collecting memorabilia in women's sports of interest to you. Memorabilia pertaining to women's sports offers tremendous growing potential as interest in women's sports should only continue to grow.

Female professional athletes have obviously come into their own on the golfing and tennis circuits. Autographs and tournament programs are two types of the memorabilia available in this field.

Otherwise, it is especially in collegiate sports where female teams are beginning to receive the spotlight.

Steps

☐ A good place to begin your hunt for memorabilia related to women's sports is with Appendix U, a partial list of colleges and universities.

☐ Write a letter to the director of the women's athletic program for information regarding memorabilia they may have available.

WOMEN'S SPORTS MEMORABILIA (continued)

Name of College/University
Address of College/University

Attn: Director of Women's Athletics

Dear Director,

I am a collector of sports-related memorabilia and am interested in women's sports. I would like to expand my collection to include memorabilia related to women's sports.

Please send me information regarding your women's team sports programs and any items, such as game programs or scorecards that you feel might make interesting collectibles. In addition, if you are aware of any women's sports organizations I could contact for additional information I would appreciate your letting me know.

For your convenience I have enclosed a stamped, self-addressed envelope. Thank you for your attention to my request. I look forward to hearing from you soon.

Signed,

Your Name
Your Address

☐ Based on information you receive regarding available items, plan a strategy of what you want to collect.

☐ Be on the lookout for new opportunities as women's sports gain more recognition and prominence.

MINOR LEAGUES

Getting Started

You never know when one of today's minor league players will become tomorrow's major league star. There is not as much team- and player-related minor league memorabilia available as in the majors, but it is becoming more plentiful as the minor league teams gain in popularity and following. For example, minor leaguer trading cards are now available. In addition, if you live or vacation where a minor league team plays, it could offer a good opportunity to accumulate autographs, game programs, scorecards, and related promotional material.

Steps

☐ Of course, as with any collection technique, try to have an idea of what you're after before you begin. Next, use the minor league team addresses found in the Appendices in the Collectors' Resources section to begin your "hit" list.

☐ You can contact the teams by mail, by telephone, or in person. Unless you have targeted available memorabilia through game attendance, the most effective method may be by mail. Write the teams you are interested in (or the team your targeted players play for) a letter such as the following to request information, specific memorabilia, or autographs.

MINOR LEAGUES (continued)

FOR INFORMATION

Team Name
Team Address

Attn: Public Relations Department

Dear Team Public Relations Department,

The (insert name of minor league team here) is one of my favorite minor league teams. In fact, I try to follow the team and its players as closely as I can and collect low-cost, team-related sports memorabilia.

Please send me any team-related information and memorabilia you think would be of interest to a fan such as myself. Please include a schedule of upcoming games, their locations, and any promotions that will be taking place. I am also interested in player autograph opportunities.

Thank you for your attention to my request. For your convenience, a large self-addressed, stamped envelope is enclosed for your response. I look forward to hearing from you soon.

Signed,

Your Name
Your Address

MINOR LEAGUES (continued)

FOR SPECIFIC MEMORABILIA (i.e., game programs)

Team Name
Team Address

Attn: Team Public Relations Department

Dear Team Public Relations Department,

I am an avid fan of (insert name of minor league team here) and collect (insert targeted specific type of memorabilia here). Is it possible to obtain this type of memorabilia directly from the team? If so, I need to know if there is a cost involved, since I have limited funds available for my collection. I would be happy to cover shipping and handling costs for the memorabilia if necessary.

Thank you for your prompt attention to my questions. Enclosed is a stamped, self-addressed envelope for your response. I look forward to hearing from you soon.

Signed,

Your Name
Your Address

MINOR LEAGUES (continued)

FOR AUTOGRAPHS

Player Name
Team Name
Team Address

Dear Name of Player,

I am a longtime fan and avid autograph collector and would welcome the opportunity to add your autograph to my collection. (Mention here whether you plan to attend an upcoming game or whether an item to autograph is enclosed.)

For your convenience, a self-addressed, stamped envelope is enclosed for your response. Thank you for your prompt response to my request. I look forward to hearing from you soon.

Signed,

Your Name
Your Address

☐ Obviously, if you regularly attend games you could try to get autographs without writing first. Please remember, though, that the players' primary function is to play ball and that catering to fans' demands is secondary.

☐ Treat players in the minors with the same courtesy you would give those in the majors. If it's possible, request the autograph in advance and be ready when it's time. Have paper and a working pen handy and make your request short and sweet.

SENIOR LEAGUES

Getting Started

The advent of Senior Leagues offer new opportunities for sports-related memorabilia.

The Senior Leagues expand the professional life of players, as well as the time period in which they can distinguish themselves with achievements. This can increase the value of memorabilia from select players' earlier playing years, as well as create a market for new memorabilia from their Senior League years.

Unfortunately, the Senior League had to fold for the 1990-91 season. Reorginazational plans are under way to reopen the league in the winter of 1991. Check with the Senior League office for up-to-date information if you want to find out more about their plans and the individual teams.

Steps

☐ As of December 1990 there were six teams in the Professional Baseball Senior League.

☐ If your target is memorabilia related to a specific player, yet you aren't sure which team he is playing for, you might consider sending a generic letter such as the following to each of the various teams. Not only will you find out where your favorite players from the past are playing, you may receive some interesting team-related facts, if not memorabilia, as well.

SENIOR LEAGUES (continued)

Team Name
Team Address

Attn: Public Relations Department

Dear Team Public Relations Department,

I find the advent of Baseball's Senior League very exciting and am interested in learning all I can about your team. In addition, I collect low-cost, sports-related memorabilia and am anxious to expand my collection into the Senior League area.

Please send me any and all information you make available for fans, such as a current team roster, scheduled games, and scheduled promotions. Enclosed is a stamped, self-addressed envelope for your convenience. Thank you for your response to my request. I look forward to hearing from you soon.

Signed,

Your Name
Your Address

☐ Once you have located your targeted players, you might write them to congratulate them on their new affiliations with Senior League teams. Mention that you collect autographs and that you would appreciate theirs. As always, enclose a stamped, self-addressed envelope and you might get your autograph by return mail.

Sports memorabilia from universities and colleges is often forgotten, but there is a lot available, especially at those schools with strong sports programs.

COLLEGIATE TEAMS

Getting Started

To some people it's flat un-American not to follow collegiate sports. Especially if you or a family member attended a college or university that has a prominent sports program, being a fan is almost instinctive. It's a natural step to want to combine this interest with your hobby of collecting sports-related memorabilia.

Some hobbyists collect college and university sports-related memorabilia exclusively. It's fun, low stress, definitely low cost, and rife with possibilities. You never know when you might luck out and acquire memorabilia related to a future professional star athlete.

Steps

☐ If you don't follow any particular collegiate teams already, Appendix U provides a partial list of addresses for some of the universities and colleges with more prominent sports programs.

☐ If you attend games, you are already in a perfect position to collect programs, scorecards, autographs, and any promotional items offered. To maximize your memorabilia collecting opportunities gameside, write a letter such as the following to the head of the sports program. (You can learn who to direct your letter to specifically with a quick phone call to the college or university itself.)

COLLEGIATE TEAMS
(continued)

Name of Athletic Director or
    Specific Team Coach
University/College Name
University/College Address

Dear Name of Director,

I am a longtime, avid fan (and mention here if alumnus as well) of (insert name of school/team here). In fact, I regularly attend games and actively collect all team-related — free and low cost — memorabilia.

Please send me a schedule of upcoming games, including any promotional items that may be available. In addition, when would you suggest as the best opportunities to obtain player autographs?

Enclosed is a self-addressed, stamped envelope for your response. Thank you for your attention to my request. I look forward to hearing from you soon. Good luck in the upcoming season!

Signed,

Your Name
Your Address

COLLEGIATE TEAMS
(continued)

☐ If you are unable to attend games of the teams that interest you, modify the above letter to read something like this:

Name of Athletic Director or
    Specific Team Coach
University/College Name
University/College Address

Dear Name of Director,

I am a longtime, avid fan (and mention here if alumnus as well) of (insert name of school/team here). In fact, I actively collect all team-related — free and low cost — memorabilia.

Please send me any information that you feel would be of interest, including the availability of unsold game programs and scorecards. In addition, is it possible to obtain player autographs by mail?

Enclosed is a self-addressed, stamped envelope for your response. Thank you for your attention to my request. I look forward to hearing from you soon. Good luck in the upcoming season!

Signed,

Your Name
Your Address

☐ Note that in many instances, collegiate sports have become more and more profit-conscious in recent years. If you truly believe in the sports programs of the schools you follow, you might consider making the cash donation, if required, for specific desired memorabilia. As always, you must decide if the memorabilia is worth the out of pocket cost.

INTERNATIONAL SPORTS

Getting Started

Every day we read how a global society is growing out of our individual nations. Much of what we do is inter-related and, as such, what one country does affects the others. Sports is also feeling the effects of globalization. A case in point are baseball and basketball players who opt to play abroad either because they lack the skills to play professionally here and wish to develop themselves further, or because they prefer the international leagues. In addition, some of our professional teams are actually scheduling off-season games in foreign countries.

Globalization offers unique new opportunities to collectors of sports-related memorabilia. If you follow specific American teams who now have games abroad, a unique piece of memorabilia could be the foreign newspaper coverage of the game. If you follow specific players, you may be able to find foreign trading cards for the years they played overseas.

Taken a step further, globalization can carry you into an entirely new area — the collection of sports-related memorabilia for certain sports worldwide. Interested in Japanese or Caribbean League baseball? How about international soccer?

You may even make new friends for your efforts. Wouldn't it be something to establish trading partners in different parts of the world? You could trade them the American sports-related memorabilia they value for the foreign sports-related memorabilia you seek. People around the world are very much like you and me once you speak a common language. Sports-related memorabilia could be that language.

Ah, but enthusiasm takes us ahead of ourselves. Although the global collecting opportunities are growing daily, for our purpose let's define where to begin.

INTERNATIONAL SPORTS (continued)

Steps

☐ There are professional sports team associations besides the familiar NFL, NHL, NBA, and National and American Baseball Leagues. A partial list can be found in Appendix S.

☐ Look at this list and select associations that represent sports of interest to you. (Even though they may be headquartered in foreign countries, most of them have English as one of their official languages.) Write those you have selected a letter such as the following.

Name of Professional Sport Association
Association Address

Attn: Public Relations Department

Dear Public Relations Department Director,

As an avid sports fan, I am interested in finding out more about your organization and the group of teams you represent. Please send information you may have available, such as team names, addresses, association statement of purpose, etc.

Enclosed is an International Reply Postal Coupon and self-addressed envelope for your response. Thank you for your attention to my request. I look forward to hearing from you soon. Good luck in the upcoming season!

Signed,

Your Name
Your Address

INTERNATIONAL SPORTS (continued)

☐ Depending on what you receive in return, you now may want to write a letter to the individual teams that interest you.

Team Name
Team Address

Attn: Public Relations Department

Dear Team Public Relations Department,

I am an avid sports fan and active collector of sports-related memorabilia. I am very interested in learning more about your team, as well as any team-related memorabilia opportunities that may be available. Please send me any material on the team you feel would be of interest.

In addition, can you tell me how I might get in touch with any of your local fans who might be interested in corresponding with me?

Thank you for your help. A self-addressed envelope and an International Postal Reply Coupon are enclosed for your response. I look forward to hearing from you soon.

Signed,

Your Name
Your Address

☐ Letters to countries outside of the United States and Canada should be sent airmail and require extra postage.

☐ Headquarters located in foreign countries cannot respond to your letters using the U.S. postage stamps you would normally include, so purchase International Postal Reply Coupons at your post office to cover the return postage.

HALLS OF FAME

Getting Started

The Halls of Fame for the respective sports are all about the stars. Their purpose is to honor those who have achieved the pinnacle in professional sportsmanship, both athletically and personally. In addition, they desire to promote the best that their respective sports have to offer the public. What a great source for memorabilia!

You can acquire memorabilia from Halls of Fame through them directly by writing or visiting, or via alternative paths that the Halls of Fame inadvertently provide access to.

Steps

☐ Appendix R gives you the addresses for the Halls of Fame for Hockey, Baseball, Basketball, and Football.

☐ Using a letter such as the following, write the Hall of Fame for the sports interesting to you to see what types of information and memorabilia they could make available at little or no cost.

HALLS OF FAME (continued)

✉

Name of Hall of Fame
Hall of Fame Address

Attn: Public Relations Department Director

Dear Public Relations Department Director,

I have followed (insert name of sport here) for many years and, of course, in the process have heard much about the Hall of Fame. However, I am unfamiliar with the services which you make available to fans. In particular, I am interested in any sports-related memorabilia you may offer, since I am an avid collector.

Please send any information you feel would be of interest to me regarding the Hall of Fame and memorabilia available. Please include any costs involved as the funds I have available are restrictive.

Enclosed is a postage paid, self-addressed envelope for your response. Thank you for your prompt assistance. I look forward to hearing from you soon.

Signed,

Your Name
Your Address

✉

☐ Of course, if you have the opportunity, visit the Halls of Fame. It would be a marvelous outing and probably net you the same information, if not more, since you could see some of the items firsthand and immediately ask any additional questions that might arise.

☐ As tourists, many people purchase memorabilia when they visit a Hall of Fame, just as they do whenever they vacation somewhere. But odds are, several years down the road, what was meant to be a memento has become unwanted clutter. For little or nothing, they may be happy to turn it over to you.

HALLS OF FAME (continued)

☐ Most Halls of Fame keep voluntary guest registers. Using a letter such as that below, write the Hall of Fame and request they send you a copy of their list of visitors from previous years. Depending on the availability of the information and the staff's time constraints, you may receive a response. Although our objective is to obtain as much free memorabilia as possible, it might tempt them to comply with your request if you enclose a donation for their trouble.

✉

Name of Hall of Fame
Hall of Fame Address

Attn: Public Relations Department Director

Dear Public Relations Department Director,

As an avid fan of (insert name of sport here) and active collector of sports-related memorabilia, I am anxious to establish contact with other fans such as myself. I would greatly appreciate a copy of any list you might keep of people who have visited the Hall of Fame over the past year or so. (This list would be for my private use only and would not be used for the purpose of selling these people anything!)

For your convenience a postage paid, self-addressed envelope is enclosed. Thank you for your attention to my request. I look forward to hearing from you soon.

Signed,

Your Name
Your Address

✉

HALLS OF FAME (continued)

☐ Should your request get results, write to previous visitors using a similar letter:

Visitor Name
Visitor Address

Dear Fellow Sports Fan,

I noticed that you visited the (insert name of sports here) Hall of Fame several years ago. I am a collector of sports-related memorabilia and wondered if you had any memorabilia that was no longer of interest to you. Please send me a description of the items and what worth, if any, you feel they have in the marketplace. Should the worth be questionable, please write me about it anyway. Depending on the item I still may be willing to pay for shipping to take it off your hands.

By the way, do you actively collect sports-related memorabilia yourself? If so, is there any particular area of concentration? I am always searching for new trading partners.

For your convenience I have enclosed a stamped, self-addressed envelope for your response. Thank you for your time. I look forward to hearing from you soon.

Signed,

Your Name
Your Address

✉

☐ Reminder: never miss an opportunity to develop a new trading partner. Not only could it lead to valuable additions for your collection, but you also may develop some interesting friendships with people you wouldn't have met otherwise.

HALLS OF FAME (continued)

☐ Should the opportunity present itself, and if you don't mind crowds, consider attending an annual inductee ceremony. You never know who will be in attendance. Even though it may be difficult to get near that year's inductees, you might be able to get autographs of other sports figures not currently in the spotlight, such as friends of current inductees and other sports personalities who enjoy attending the event.

☐ If you miss a targeted player at the inductee ceremonies, use it as an opportunity to contact the player in writing using a letter such as the one below, requesting an autograph or other sort of memorabilia of interest to you. By the way, since you may not have access to the player's private home address, write him in care of the most recent team with whom he played, using the team address lists in the Appendices. Often the team will forward the letter appropriately on your behalf.

Many fans like to have collecting cards such as these autographed by the players.

HALLS OF FAME (continued)

Name of Player
Player Address

Dear Name of Player,

Congratulations on your recent induction into the Hall of Fame! I had the great thrill of being at the ceremony to witness your induction; however, I missed the opportunity to meet with you.

I have been a fan of yours since (mention an approximate year or event that brought the player to your attention). Ever since I have actively followed your career and collected memorabilia related to it. If it would not be too much trouble I would appreciate your autograph on the enclosed item (or substitute whatever other request you may have).

Especially in light of your recent honor, I am sure there are many other demands on your time, but any way you could find to fulfill my request would be appreciated. For your convenience a postage paid, self-addressed envelope is enclosed. Thank you for your time. I look forward to hearing from you soon.

Signed,

Your Name
Your Address

If you are unable to attend the ceremony at the Hall of Fame, eliminate the second sentence of paragraph 1 and send the same letter.

BY MAIL

Getting Started

Autographs don't have to be hard to obtain. Both active and retired players frequently will respond to your autograph request if you write directly to them. Sound too simple? It is. But it can work.

Players respond to written autograph requests for several reasons. Of course, it's good PR and often players are flattered by your interest. After all, without fans like you their names and playing records would be forgotten. It is also easier for players to respond to written autograph requests versus the mob scenes that occur during personal appearances, since they can sign items at their convenience.

Steps

☐ Write individual letters such as the one that follows to the players from whom you desire autographs.

✉

Player Name
Team Name and Address

Dear Player Name,

I am a longtime fan and active collector of sports-related memorabilia. I would greatly appreciate your autograph on the enclosed (name of enclosed item to be autographed) for my collection.

A self-addressed, stamped envelope is enclosed for your convenience. Thank you very much for donating your time and energy to this request. I look forward to your response.

Signed,

Your Name
Your Address

✉

BY MAIL (continued)

☐ For players who are still playing professionally, send your letter in care of their current team. (Team addresses for all professional baseball, basketball, football, and hockey teams are provided in the Appendices.)

☐ For retired players, send your letter in care of the team he predominantly played with during his career. In most cases the club will forward your letter to the player.

☐ You will have a better chance of having your autograph-by-mail requests fulfilled if you enclose just one or two items for signature. Players have become leery of anyone who appears to be requesting their autographs for potential resale rather than as a true fan. Be patient in waiting for a response. Remember, players have their own lives and you are imposing on their time to do this.

☐ You should consult, and possibly may want to buy, Buck Kronnick's book, *The Baseball Fan's Complete Guide to Collecting Autographs*, published by Betterway Publications, Inc. In addition to some excellent tips on obtaining autographs, it includes listings of the home addresses (current as of the publication date) and birthdates for all those living who ever played major league baseball.

AT THE GAME

Getting Started

Some players only autograph at the games. What a great excuse to have to attend! This is a good way to get larger items such as a ball or game program signed.

Realizing that the player's job is to play the game, the best time to approach him is either during pre-game warm-ups or after the game by standing outside the player entrance/exit. Don't push yourself on the players. Introduce yourself as a loyal fan and ask if this is a convenient time. Treat players as you would like to be treated and you should get good results.

Steps

☐ Contact team headquarters before the game and ask when and how they would recommend that you request autographs at the game. They may be uncooperative or they may have some time-saving tips.

☐ Plan your strategy before you go. Decide whose autographs you would like to acquire, what you'd like signed, and when you are going to attempt to make player contact.

☐ This step is the most important and makes this type of autograph collecting the most fun. ATTEND THE GAME!

☐ Bring only one item to be autographed. Too many items may be too large of an imposition and discourage the player from signing anything for you.

☐ Be at the appointed place at the appointed time and have a writing utensil that writes easily!

VIA FAN MAIL

Getting Started

There are few people in this world who don't appreciate a sincere compliment. Celebrities are no different. Even if they are pleased with their performance, they continue to wonder how they are perceived by the public. Ultimately, the longevity of their careers is tied to the public's desire to see them in action.

If there is a player or coach who you admire, or you feel deserves a pat on the back for something they have done, let them know this by writing them. When you write out of sincerity instead of as a ploy to get something in return, you will be amazed at the frequency with which the sports personalities will write you a personal note in response to your kindness. Of course, the signature on their letter is an autograph, but they often are only too happy to supply this to you in appreciation for what you have done.

Steps

☐ You could write them with: congratulations for the player having achieved a personal goal you were aware of, a birthday card with special comments about why you admire their work, words of encouragement or reaffirming your belief in them even when their recent track record or the media seems to speak against them, feelings of condolence in times of their personal tragedies, etc. It can be for any number of things as long as it is written from your heart and not your collector's avarice.

☐ Unlike when you write to request an autograph, you are requesting nothing. You are giving them freely of yourself and your time. Often they feel this warrants a response. Not every person you write will respond. Only use this technique when you really are doing it for the benefit of the player — when the autograph is not the priority. Phoniness comes across immediately in writing. Be tolerant of their time to respond. We have received responses as long as eighteen months after we sent our letter.

VIA FAN MAIL (continued)

☐ If you do not have the player's private home address at your disposal, send your letter in care of their current team. (Team addresses for all professional baseball, basketball, football, and hockey teams are provided in the Appendices.) For retired players, send your letter in care of the team he played predominantly with during his career. In most cases the club will forward your letter to the player.

BOOKSTORES/PUBLISHERS

Getting Started

In recent years, celebrity tell-all biographies have been some of the bestselling books. The public can't seem to get enough of current celebrities' private lives, including sports celebrities. There are no signs of this recent trend abating and this provides an opportunity for collectors such as yourself, especially autograph collectors.

Should your collection emphasize a player who is the subject of a book, owning it enhances your collection. Books themselves can even become collectible items. They often include many photos of the sports celebrity and, depending on the popularity of the book itself, there may or may not be many books sold, possibly qualifying the book as a rarity years after it was published.

In addition, to promote a recently issued book, publishers often schedule a tour for the author to make appearances and sign autographs. Even though it is often a ghostwriter who does the actual writing and the celebrity who just provides the tale to be told, it is the celebrity the public wants to see and the celebrity who goes on tour.

Steps

☐ Whenever you are in your local bookstore, ask whether the bookseller is aware of any books due out in the near future that are biographies of sports personalities. If the response is affirmative, see if they can get you the name and address of the publisher. Then write a letter such as the following to try to receive a copy of the author's book signing tour.

BOOKSTORES/PUBLISHERS (continued)

✉

Publishing Co. Name
Publishing Co. Address

Attn: Promotions Department

Dear (Publishing Co. Name)
Promotions Department,

It has come to my attention that your company will be publishing a book by and/or about (name of sports personality) in the near future. I am an avid fan of (name of sports personality) and am anxious to have the opportunity to consider the book for purchase as well as have a copy autographed by (name of sports personality).

Please let me know when and where you are planning personal appearances by (name of sports personality) for autographs to promote the book. For your convenience I have enclosed a self-addressed, stamped envelope for your response.

Thank you for your attention to my request. I look forward to hearing from you soon.

Signed,

Your Name
Your Address

✉

☐ Attend autograph sessions of interest to you and when you do, remember to get there early. It is likely that the player will be bombarded by signature requests if the book signing has been as well-publicized as it should. To show courtesy to the player, buy a copy of the book to be signed instead of having the player autograph anything else. Your purchase shows true support and consideration for why the player is giving his or her time to autograph. Of course, an autographed copy of the book is more likely to become a valuable piece of memorabilia in its own right as well.

BOOKSTORES/PUBLISHERS (continued)

☐ Collectors who are serious about following the release of sports personality-related books should use *Publisher's Weekly* as an important information source. This weekly magazine is the bible of the publishing industry. Among other things it reports on and has advertisements for upcoming books prior to their release, including information on the publisher. *Publisher's Weekly* is available at many libraries. (Subscription costs would rarely be warranted given the limited amount of relevant books released each year.)

☐ Of course, if there is no signing near to you, you could always buy the book and then send the book via the publisher or team to the player for signature with a letter such as the following. The fact that you purchased the book gives the player incentive to sign. Of course, be sure to include a self-addressed, stamped (with proper postage) box for the book to be returned to you to make it easy for the player to comply with your request.

BOOKSTORES/PUBLISHERS (continued)

Name of Player
c/o Team or Publisher Name
Team or Publisher Address

Dear Name of Player,

I was pleased to be able to purchase a copy of your recently issued book, (insert name of book here).

I am an avid fan and have followed your career with interest since (try to name approximate year or event that first brought the player to your attention). As such, I am also an active collector of related memorabilia and would value nothing more than having my copy of your book autographed.

In the event you could find the time to fill my request, I have enclosed the book for your signature. Should my request prove too great an imposition, please return it to me. Regardless, a postage-paid, self-addressed box to return the book in is enclosed for your convenience.

Thank you for your time. I look forward to hearing from you soon and wish you continued success in your future endeavors.

Signed,

Your Name
Your Address

SPRING TRAINING

Getting Started

A visit to a team's spring training site can provide the opportunity for unique autographs. During spring training many more players are involved than finally participate during the regular season. Like dealing with the minor leagues, autographs from some now lesser-known players could reap large benefits if they find greater success in the big leagues as they mature as players. If you don't live near your favorite team's spring home, what a great excuse for a vacation to sunny lands!

Steps

☐ To get the most out of your visit to spring training — PLAN AHEAD! Recently, teams have been actively marketing their spring training games. The result is greater crowds, which means more competition for those seeking autographs and other related memorabilia.

☐ Maximize your efforts by making a target list of the players whose autographs are most important to you and include notations regarding how you propose to get the autographs.

☐ It may pay to write a letter preceding your visit to request information about recommended times and places to meet players and get autographs. The letter could be addressed to one specific player or to the team public relations department, depending on the focus of your autograph collection. Samples follow:

SPRING TRAINING (continued)

TO SPECIFIC PLAYER

✉

Player Name
Team Name
Team Address

Dear (insert name of player here),

Ever since (insert approximate year or event that brought player to your attention), I have been an avid fan. In fact, I actively collect memorabilia related to your career. I have the opportunity to visit your spring training camp around (insert estimated date of visit) and wondered when might be a convenient opportunity to meet you and get your autograph.

I realize that your time is limited, but would appreciate any few minutes you could offer. Enclosed is a postage-paid, self-addressed envelope for your response. I look forward to hearing from you soon. Good luck in the upcoming season! Here's one fan who's behind you all the way.

Signed,

Your Name
Your Address

✉

SPRING TRAINING (continued)

TO TEAM PUBLIC RELATIONS
DEPARTMENT

✉

Team Name
Team Address

Attn: Team Public Relations Department

Dear Team Public Relations Department,

I am an avid team fan. In fact, this spring I have the unique opportunity to attend some spring training games.

As an active collector of team-related memorabilia (especially autographs), are there specific times and places you would recommend I approach players for their autographs during spring training? I plan on being in the spring training camp area around (insert approximate time of visit here).

Your assistance is greatly appreciated. A stamped, self-addressed envelope is enclosed for your response. Thank you for your attention to my request. I look forward to hearing from you soon and meeting the players this spring.

Signed,

Your Name
Your Address

✉

☐ Most often you will want to send your letters to the team's year-round headquarters (See Appendices).

☐ Appendix B includes listings of recent locations of baseball spring training camps for individual teams.

☐ Look in Appendix W as well for a list of sports-related periodicals. Frequently, prior to the beginning of spring training, many of these will feature articles on upcoming off-season training.

PLAYER PUBLIC APPEARANCES

Getting Started

Teams are profit-oriented, commercial ventures. Without a public who enthusiastically follows it to pay for game tickets and support television advertisement revenues, the team cannot exist. For this reason, maintenance of a highly visible, good public image is very important to every team.

Part of their "public relations" strategy often includes scheduled appearances where the public can meet the players. Sometimes these are coordinated to support local charities at the same time. If you know when and where which players are to appear, you could make arrangements for some super autograph opportunities.

Steps

☐ Write a letter such as the following to team PR department to request a schedule of player public appearances in your area.

Team Name
Team Address

Attn: Team Public Relations Department

Dear Team Public Relations Department,

I live in the (insert the large recognizable community you belong in) area. As a longtime, loyal fan of the team I would be interested in knowing when any public appearances may be scheduled in my area. I welcome any opportunity to meet the players and receive their autographs.

Please send me a schedule of upcoming player public appearances. Thank you for your assistance. For your convenience a postage-paid, self-addressed envelope is enclosed. I look forward to hearing from you soon.

Signed,

Your Name
Your Address

PLAYER PUBLIC APPEARANCES (continued)

☐ You could even write ahead of time to a player you are interested in and inform him you are interested in his autograph. However, the merit of this strategy is questionable at best. Keep in mind that during the public appearance it would be difficult for the player to separate you from the rest of the crowd, let alone give you preferential treatment.

☐ Once you become aware of a scheduled public appearance, ARRIVE EARLY and BE PREPARED! Out of courtesy have only one item for the player to autograph. When you arrive at the front of the line, have it in your hand, along with a pen that you are certain will write on the item.

☐ Sometimes a player public appearance is scheduled at a charity function. Since the nature of the function is generally to be a fundraiser, there is often a charge to get in. If you do not wish to pay the entrance fee, volunteer to help the local charity at the event. Let them know that your purpose is two-fold: help the charity and meet a player you admire. Ask if there is something you could do that would give you the opportunity to meet the player. Of course, if you volunteered to work, don't shirk your duty. This strategy is only effective when it helps all involved: you get in free to get your autograph and the charity receives needed help.

☐ If opportunity doesn't knock on your door, you could always try to create opportunity yourself. Should there be no public appearances scheduled in your area in the near future, perhaps you could help make arrangements for one. A local charity you are involved with may benefit from the added draw a sports personality would bring to an upcoming fundraiser. Offer to be the person who contacts the team public relations department to try to set it up. If you are successful, you might even be the charity's welcoming committee when the athlete arrives.

TRADE YOUR DUPLICATES

Getting Started

Since the dawn of time sports card collectors have traded their duplicates for cards they wanted for their collections. Trading duplicates for memorabilia you want prevents out-of-pocket costs, enhances your collection, and establishes contacts with other collectors, which may prove valuable.

Steps

There are several ways to trade your duplicates, including

☐ Attend a collectors' show. Watch for notices in your local newspaper of upcoming sports-related memorabilia shows. When you sign in at the first one they often ask you to specify whether you would like to be informed of future shows. Great! You're on the mailing list. In addition, periodicals such as *Sports Collectors' Digest* do a great job of listing collectors' shows held nationwide so you can find the ones closest to you. Consult the partial list of periodicals found in Appendix W.

☐ Advertise in sports publications. For a very low cost you can let tens of thousands of other collectors know you are in the market to trade. Look in Appendix W for a partial list of publications. A sample ad could read:
BRAVES wanted. Trade even for your team, old or new. Send cards guaranteed.

☐ Visit dealers. Consult your local telephone directory Yellow Pages. Look under topics such as "Hobby," "Baseball," or "Collectibles" for local dealers near you. Using your want list, your inventory, and a knowledge of going prices, negotiate for the best deals.

☐ Write dealers who advertise in sports publications. (There is a partial list of sports periodicals in Appendix W.) Send them a list of what you have and what you need.

☐ Don't overlook your duplicate commons. Although these may be of little monetary value alone, they may prove of high trading value with other collectors. Many collectors preserve known star cards, but common cards often are discarded in the early years. This makes it difficult for collectors to complete sets in later years.

As this ad demonstrates, dealers are looking to buy from you as well as sell to you, providing you with ready cash to purchase the items you can't acquire for free.

BARTERING
Getting Started

Can you do something others think is great, which others need to have done? If so you have the means of expanding your collection using the oldest method of exchange in the world — bartering.

Long before there was money, there was bartering. Bartering is defined as to trade by exchanging one item for another. This is different from a sale or purchase, where money is paid for the items transferred between a buyer and seller. Even if you don't have other sports-related memorabilia you are willing to trade, you can trade your labor or a skill you possess, something you make or do, for desired memorabilia.

Steps

☐ Make a list of what skills, talents, or abilities you may have that could be of help to others.

☐ Let it be known in areas convenient to you that in return for whatever type of collectible you seek, you will do ... gardening, mowing lawns, repair work, build, etc.

☐ You can publicize your services any number of ways, including by distribution of flyers on a regular basis, walking door to door, or placing an ad in the local newspaper (although this last option will cost).

☐ Remember, your intent is to trade your services for the sports-related memorabilia you seek. If there is more than labor involved in the services you will be doing, i.e., costs for materials, make sure the customer understands he must supply everything besides your time for completion of the work. In order to accomplish your objective of acquiring the memorabilia you desire at little or no cost, your only investment should be the donation of your time.

☐ Of course, remain reasonable. If someone offers you a monetarily valuable piece of memorabilia in return for one of the dog houses you make in your garage as a side business, consider the value of what's being offered before demanding the customer pay for the wood and nails.

BARTERING (continued)

☐ Even if a potential customer offers you sports-related memorabilia that is not a high priority on your want list, do not discount the customer's offer immediately. Never overlook an opportunity to pick up collectibles you can use to trade for things you ultimately want.

☐ Put your agreement in writing and have both parties sign and date it before you perform the service to lessen the possibility of future misunderstandings.

ATTICS

Getting Started

Antique collectors have long known that America's attics can yield treasures. They are just as likely to yield sports-related memorabilia treasures as anything else. Now, not every attic has riches waiting to be discovered, but you can increase your chances by doing a little demographic research and concentrating your attic treasure hunting on homes in areas most likely to yield the greatest results.

Attics with the most likely memorabilia potential are those in the homes of adults who still live in the home where they raised their children. If the parents have relocated, chances are the attic treasures you seek were moved to the grown child's home or thrown out.

Frequently, a child, who at one time was an avid memorabilia collector, at a certain age will have lost interest. If the memorabilia didn't immediately land in an attic box, it was most likely moved there once the child went off to college or left home for a job or marriage. In many cases, that is where the memorabilia still remains.

Cleaning out the attic is rarely at the top of anyone's list of things they want to do. Sometimes they wish they could just hire someone to go through it. While you may not demand money, you might lay claim to any sports-related memorabilia you find in the process.

Steps

☐ Of course your first attic visit should be to your own parents in case you have not already recovered the forgotten treasures of your childhood years.

☐ Do not delay in this seemingly obvious step because you take for granted that Dear Mom and Dad will forever store your goods. There are unlimited stories of memorabilia collectors who forgot the memorabilia they had accumulated as children. When they finally got around to trying to recover it, they discovered Mom and Dad, tired of being the nearest Public Storage, had discarded all unclaimed items years before.

ATTICS (continued)

☐ Next, seek out those neighborhoods where you see a potentially large population of households that fit the "attic memorabilia treasure potential" criteria. Offer to clean out and organize their attics for little or no fee. In return you wish the right to keep any sports-related memorabilia you find during your work.

☐ Now this technique only works if you actually have a flare for organizing or are willing to acquire the skill. The purpose is to offer a service the customer wants in return for the compensation you prefer.

☐ Unharnessed creativity and common courtesy should provide the foundation for developing your own unique methods of soliciting "attic organization for treasure" exchanges. Among others, three ways to solicit interest in your Free Attic Cleaning Service include: walking door to door, dropping flyers regularly at each residence, or having your local church or other group announce your service in their bulletin.

☐ Remember that seniors especially are interested in services that will make their lives easier and eliminate unpleasant tasks from their list of chores. In addition, grown children who are helping their parents move may more than welcome your offer. Be careful to spell out what the customer should and should not expect.

☐ Clean and organize your own attic first to provide a practice run-through. It will give you an idea of the difficulties you may face, as well as help you define what services you are actually capable of performing.

☐ As you clean, organize, and search for buried treasure in a customer's attic be aware that you are rummaging around in others' personal things. If there is any question whether or not the customer would want to keep an item or not, ASK. Don't be surprised if your customer even wishes to look over your shoulder as you work. Yes, the customer might seem a crusty curmudgeon, but could become a loving new friend if handled correctly.

ATTICS (continued)

☐ Although it can seem nice to keep arrangements informal, you and your customer should sign and date a piece of paper that describes the services you intend to provide and what you are to receive in return. This lessens the chance for future misunderstandings, like when you find that Mickey Mantle card and the customer suddenly says, "I meant all sports-related memorabilia except that."

☐ In fact, if you plan on using this technique extensively to improve your collection, you should have an attorney's counsel to help you draft your customer agreement. The attorney can also caution you as to any other potential liabilities that could arise out of your trying to do your customer and yourself a good turn.

☐ By the way, this technique works on basements and wherever else a person might store their "stuff" long-term too!

You never know what treasures lie waiting to be discovered in attics.

GIFTS
Getting Started

This is probably one of the easiest and most profitable techniques of all.

Family and friends are a great source of free memorabilia. Every year for certain holidays, birthdays, and special occasions, it is customary to exchange gifts. Nothing makes a gift-giver happier than knowing they have given you what you really wanted. If certain sports-related memorabilia is at the top of your list, let family members and friends know. (Of course, common courtesy dictates that you request items that would be affordable gifts for them.) Your updated want list makes this easy. Use of the want list with family and friends allows you to acquire some of the memorabilia that is otherwise not available free to yourself.

For example, every year my wife gave her brother-in-law sweaters for Christmas. They were nice sweaters and he was always gracious, but the gifts never seemed to hit the mark. Recently, she heard him mention in conversation that as a longtime baseball fan, as a child he had also been an avid collector of baseball trading cards. In an effort to hopefully give him some feelings of nostalgia, one Christmas she bought him the Fleer's baseball trading card set for that year. She hoped he would get a kick out of it. Instead, he was absolutely thrilled. It was one of his favorite gifts. He expressed how he loved baseball cards, but how no one ever gave him any. If he had had a want list she wouldn't have had to guess if cards were appropriate and whether Fleer's was acceptable. Now he provides us with a want list each year. He gets a gift he really wants and we know we've given a gift that will bring joy. You can do the same.

Steps

☐ Using your want list, select items you would probably be unable to acquire on your own, but are definitely within the budget of those who wish to give you gifts. Let them know what you'd like from your want list and where they can get it.

☐ Don't tell everyone to get you the same thing or you waste everyone's time and money!

SELF-SPONSORED GARAGE SALES

Getting Started

Sure, you can attend garage sales as a potential customer, but how about sponsoring a garage sale to earn money selling collectibles you no longer want, to buy collectibles you *do* want.

Steps

☐ Identify sports-related memorabilia that no longer suits the purposes of your collection. These are items to sell at your garage sale.

☐ Place a classified ad in your local newspaper, notifying readers that you are having a sports-related memorabilia garage sale. (Yes, this will result in an out-of-pocket expense unless you can figure out a creative way to barter for your ad space.)

☐ Hopefully your ad should attract other collectors to your sale who will want to buy some of your "stuff." Decide ahead of time whether you will accept personal checks in addition to cash, although *cash only* is an easier policy.

☐ Make sure you offer garage sale prices. Remember that people come to a garage sale for a good deal. The prices should benefit all — buyers should get products they want at realistic prices and you should rid yourself of unwanted memorabilia so that you have space and money for memorabilia you do want.

☐ If you are fortunate, your sports-related memorabilia garage sale could net you more than immediate cash. It could very possibly put you in contact with other area collectors you could trade with or even jointly sponsor the next sports-related memorabilia garage sale.

☐ Besides an on-site garage sale, you could also sponsor a "Mail Order Garage Sale." Advertise in a periodical like *Sports Collectors' Digest*, whose readership by definition consists of collectors like yourself. Offer them a list of items for sale in exchange for their postage-paid, self-addressed envelope. Just like their on-the-spot counterparts, mail order garage sales could net you cash, trading partners, and friends.

TRADING PALS

Getting Started

As we've already established, you have limited time and resources to enhance your collection (or you wouldn't be interested in this book). With an up-to-date want list and inventory in hand you are ready to develop trading pals. Trading pals are simply other collectors. Like you the trading pals you develop will have limited time and money to dedicate to the hobby, yet ideally their collecting efforts will have a slightly different focus. Perhaps you collect baseball memorabilia and your pal collects football; or your collection emphasizes the Braves and your pal's the Royals. The point is that as a result of your collecting efforts you probably both have items that the other considers of greater value and worth a trade.

The potential long-term benefits of trading pals for your collection should not be overlooked. Through the informal trading networks you develop with your pals you gain access to numerous items on your want list, which would be otherwise unavailable on a low cost/no cost basis. One trading pal could conceivably lead you to others, and so on and so forth.

As long as you remain aware of what you want, what you have, and how each are fairly valued, you can only benefit from working with your trading pals.

Steps

☐ You may develop one or a variety of different trading pals.

☐ Trading pals can be people you live close enough to so that you can visit regularly or people you stay in contact with by mail.

☐ There are unlimited ways of finding and developing trading pals. The number one step is to LET PEOPLE KNOW YOU ARE LOOKING FOR OTHER COLLECTORS TO TRADE WITH!

Trading pals are in a win-win situation. Both get what they want most for their collections at little or no cost.

TRADING PALS (continued)

☐ Potential sources of trading pals include:

    Notice on bulletin board at work

    Flyer distributed around neighborhood

    Electronic bulletin boards accessed via personal computers

    Friends and relatives

    Business associates and/or their friends

    Ad placement in local sports-related periodical

    Mention your interest to your local retail dealers, who might already know of others

    Talk it up with other collectors you meet at trade shows.

    Write the president of team fan clubs and see if they will announce in an upcoming club publication who you are and that you are looking for sports-related memorabilia trading pals.

☐ Upon locating a potential trading pal, get the relationship off on the right foot by exchanging inventories and want lists. Right away you'll be able to see where, how, and if you will be able to help one another.

☐ In casual conversation with a potential new trading pal, try to learn how serious they are about their sports-related memorabilia collecting. The best matches in trading pals are between those with similar objectives. If either one of you takes the collecting too seriously or too lightly in the other's eyes, it could be harmful to the relationship.

☐ Enjoy the opportunity trading pal relationships give you to get to know new collectors.

TRADING CLUBS

Getting Started

If you are looking to combine expansion of your sports-related memorabilia collection with a little socializing, consider beginning a trading club. Unlike fan clubs, the purpose of a trading club is to group fans of *different* teams, who all share a common interest in collecting sports-related memorabilia. Ideally the collections of trading club members will emphasize different aspects of the hobby. That way, often there will be opportunities for club members to trade items less valuable to them to other members seeking those items, in return for collectibles they want.

Steps

☐ Trading clubs can be established locally or by mail. Local clubs do offer the added advantage of giving fellow collectors the opportunity to socialize with each other now and then while members trade amongst themselves to maximize their individual collections.

☐ Clubs can be small or large. The important thing is the shared interest in collecting some sort of sports-related memorabilia, and sensitivity to fair pricing on all sides of a transaction.

☐ Local clubs can begin as informally as bringing together various collectors you have come to know who live close to you. As your circle of contacts grows and as the circles of contacts of your respective members grow, so grows the participation in your club.

☐ Don't forget to let your local dealers know you're beginning a trading club. They may know of potential members right off the bat.

☐ If you want to get off to a more aggressive start, you might consider advertising, either with some sort of neighborhood flyer, the office bulletin board, or the local newspaper, to attract fellow collectors of sports-related memorabilia.

TRADING CLUBS (continued)

☐ Unless your club becomes very large, often meetings can rotate between different members' homes and refreshments, if any, can be potluck. This minimizes any out-of-pocket cost for club membership.

☐ Mandatory for all members should be a regular submission of an updated want list and inventory to other members, so that trading efforts are maximized.

☐ Use letters to presidents of team fan clubs and to the teams themselves to generate interest in a Mail Only Trading Club.

☐ If you can tolerate the cost of advertising, consider placing ads in periodicals for sports-related memorabilia collectors (see partial list in Appendix W) to find membership for your Mail Only Trading Club.

☐ Though your potential for gaining a diverse collecting membership is greater, the logistics of a Mail Only Trading Club can be a little more difficult. There will be additional costs due to the postage (and possibly long distance phone bills) necessary to execute trades with fellow members.

☐ As with any club or affiliation the most important rule to follow is K.I.S.S. (Keep It Simple Stupid!) The club should be a source of handy affiliations to ease trading, not of steady aggravation. Treat fellow members with common courtesy and remember your common goal of fulfilling your want lists with minimal time and money, and the trading club could become one of your more beneficial efforts.

COLLECTIBLE EXCHANGES

Getting Started

Is there money in your attic? How about in your basement or on your bookshelves? Do you have NON-sports-related collectibles lying around, which are of little or no interest to you, but which might be of value to another collector? Exchange them for sports-related memorabilia you do want, or sell them to raise cash to purchase the more expensive items on your want list, which you have been otherwise unable to obtain.

Steps

☐ If you formerly were an avid collector in another area, you may have friends or acquaintances who still collect. Contact them first, to see what they might be willing to offer you for your non-sports-related collectibles. (Generally, striking a deal with a fellow collector — instead of selling to a retail dealer — will net you more, since dealers have to purchase your items at a price low enough to allow for their profit when items are marked up for resale.)

☐ Know your prices before you attempt to negotiate! You want to maximize what you receive in return for your non-sports-related collectibles, however, you must also remain realistic.

☐ Visit trade shows for collectors of non-sports-related items in an attempt to find dealers or get to know attendees who might be in the market for your goods.

☐ Learn about these trade shows by watching your local newspaper or reviewing announcements and advertisements in the periodicals written for collectors of the items you wish to cash in.

☐ If you are unaware of which trade periodicals to consult, either contact local retail dealers of this type of collectible or visit your local library reference desk. The reference librarian may be able to steer you immediately to the periodical of interest to you. If not, many libraries carry a copy of guides to periodicals, which reference all types of periodicals printed.

COLLECTIBLE EXCHANGES (continued)

☐ Contact local dealers of the collectibles you wish to be rid of and ask them to make a bid.

☐ Consider advertising in the periodicals read by those who collect the specific type of collectible you wish to sell or exchange. (Of course, this alternative will probably cost you some money. You decide if the cost of the ad is worth the potential proceeds from your collectibles.)

☐ The more people who know that you're in the market to sell or exchange these other items, the better your chances of finding someone with whom to strike an all-around good deal. Don't forget to mention what you're up to in casual conversation. If people are interested, they'll pick up on it and pursue the topic with you. If not, drop it until another opportunity arises. (You don't want to make a pest of yourself either.)

☐ Never overlook the chance to trade as well as sell. You never know when you'll find an avid stamp collector who wants to add your stamps to his or her collection, in exchange for the baseball cards he or she collected as a child and hasn't touched since.

TRADE SHOWS

Getting Started

Even if you don't have extra money to spend jingling in your pockets, trade shows are fun to attend. There's excitement in the air as vendors seek to hawk their wares at a profitable price while attendees go in search of the perfect deal. And attendance of trade shows can be productive to your collecting efforts in many ways. You can talk trades with dealers and fellow attendees, find trading pals, scope out potential resale trading values, and do general research.

By their name — "trade" shows — you already know that their purpose is to bring buyers and sellers together. But even if you aren't always a buyer or a seller, the act of bringing greater numbers of buyers and sellers together under one roof at one time, makes successful trade shows the place to get a quick pulse of the hobby. Talk to dealers manning booths, listen to the conversations of other attendees and you will instantly get a feel for what's hot, what's not, and in what direction prices are trending. In addition, the potential for making new trading contacts is never better.

Steps

☐ You can't go to a show if you don't know it's in town. Step One is to find out when and where shows take place.

☐ If you already attend trade shows, watch for a sign-in sheet the next time you go. Then you can get on a mailing list for future shows.

☐ Watch your local newspaper for announcements of upcoming trade shows.

☐ Ask local dealers (who often rent booths at trade shows) which shows they patronize. They may even be able to supply you with a schedule since there's always a chance you might drop by and make a purchase at their booth.

TRADE SHOWS (continued)

☐ Periodicals for collectors of sports-related memorabilia often run advertisements and announcements of upcoming shows. Watch for those near you. If you don't subscribe to one of these periodicals already, consult the partial list of sports-related periodicals in Appendix W. Visit your local library to see if they have recent issues you can review for trade show information.

☐ Libraries also sometimes have reference guides to associations. Look up the names and descriptions of associations that seem to have something to do with sports-related memorabilia. Then write to the president of the association to find out whether they sponsor any trade shows you might be interested in attending.

Name of Association
Association Address

Attn: Association President

Dear (insert name of association here)
President,

   I am an active collector of sports-related memorabilia. Does your association sponsor any trade shows, conventions, etc. that you feel might be beneficial for me to attend?

   Please send me any information available on programs that you offer, which you feel would be of interest to me. A postage-paid, self-addressed envelope is enclosed for your response. Thank you for your attention to my request. I look forward to hearing from you soon.

Signed,

Your Name
Your Address

TRADE SHOWS (continued)

☐ Pick the shows you want to visit and schedule them on your calendar. (It may pay to call the organizers of the show before you go to confirm any cost involved for attendees.)

☐ Set objectives for what you hope to accomplish by attending a particular show. Your objective might be to meet at least one potential trading partner or to trade certain items no longer of interest to you so that you can acquire specific items on your want list. Or, your objective for some shows might be to have no objective at all other than to go for the fun of it.

☐ Take copies of your want list and inventory with you to all trade shows. You may have opportunities to trade with other attendees as well as with dealers, but before you open your mouth to begin negotiations, make sure you know what you want and how much you are willing to give up for it.

☐ Once at the shows keep your eyes and ears open to opportunity. You never know when any one of a number of possibilities will present itself.

☐ Trade, sell, and buy at trade shows, but don't hawk your wares to the general attendance like a vendor unless you've rented a booth. Work discretely, quietly, and one-on-one.

☐ Not all trade shows are successful, have worthwhile dealers manning booths, and have high attendance. Within a year or so of making the trade show circuit, you'll know which ones are worth revisiting when they come back to town.

CLASSIFIED ADS — DEALER INCENTIVES

Getting Started

Even if you're not in the market to buy, review the classified ads of sports publications for special offers. Often, in exchange for your response to an advertiser's offer of information, they will send along a "freebie."

The process benefits everyone. You receive a free gift and dealers are given the chance to introduce their services to you - a potential buyer who is likely to be interested in their goods, if not now, then later.

An example of the types of ads you may find follows:

FREE GIFT

With request for our price list on rookies and stars. Please include self-addressed stamped envelope. Send to: . . .

Steps

☐ Review the partial list of sports publications provided for you in Appendix W. If you don't already subscribe, often you can review copies of these publications free of charge at your local library.

☐ Review the classified sections of these publications on an ongoing basis for ads similar to the example above.

☐ Use a quick note such as the one below to respond to those ads that interest you, and receive your free gifts:

CLASSIFIED ADS — DEALER INCENTIVES (continued)

Advertiser Name
Advertiser Address

Dear Advertiser Name,

Per your ad in (insert publication name here), Please send the information and free gift advertised to:

Your Name
Your Address

As instructed a self-addressed, stamped envelope is enclosed. Thank you for your prompt attention to this request.

Signed,

Your Name
Your Address

☐ Should the time come in the future that you decide to make some purchases, remember the dealers who advertised and supplied you with free gifts. If their prices and product quality are competitive, consider giving them your business in appreciation.

NEWSPAPERS

Getting Started

Local teams get lots of local news coverage. When a team does especially well, newspapers frequently print their own team memorabilia for readers.

For example, each time the San Francisco Giants or the Oakland Athletics have won their pennant, one local newspaper has printed a page-size poster covered with individual "cards" of team players.

Steps

☐ When your local team achieves a significant accomplishment, contact the newspapers to see whether they will be producing any special collectors' sections or editions.

☐ Should you collect memorabilia for a team outside your area, contact the team's office headquarters or their local Chamber of Commerce for the names of the newspapers most likely to provide special event coverage.

☐ Call these newspapers and ask the Sports Department how you can get copies of their special sections or editions.

☐ Due to the time element involved (special editions by nature of newspapers appear quickly following the team's event or accomplishment), call newspapers instead of writing whenever possible. By the time they respond to your letter it will most likely be too late.

SPORTS PUBLICATION PROPRIETARY MEMORABILIA

Getting Started

If you are a card collector you are liable to pick up a copy of periodicals such as *Baseball Card Price Guide* once in awhile, just to keep abreast of your collection's potential resale value. You may receive an added bonus. Periodicals are always looking for ways to increase sales. Sometimes a promotion will include proprietary cards. For example, *Baseball Card Price Guide* has been known to bind into their publication complimentary cards that duplicate those in popular older sets.

Steps

☐ If you already subscribe to these periodicals then the collectibles sometimes enclosed are a welcome bonus to your subscription.

☐ Even if the proprietary memorabilia is not suitable for your collection, it gives you material for trading with others.

☐ If you do not subscribe, visit the library and local bookstores to keep your eye on the various publications available to identify those issues you'll want to purchase. (A partial list of sports publications is found in Appendix W.)

☐ For a quick freebie, write a letter to the periodicals you are interested in, requesting a sample copy of their publication. Many periodicals will comply with your request. It gives them a chance to present themselves to a potential future subscriber. And you might just get lucky and find some nice memorabilia waiting for you within an issue's covers.

☐ P.S. the "freebie" strategy only works once!

☐ Several of the periodicals that are written specifically to cover the collecting side of sports are invaluable resources to you and well may be worth the subscription price. Make sure you review several copies of the periodicals you like best before you take the plunge. You want to be very selective in your choices. Once again, this book assumes you have limited money to pay for subscriptions, as well as limited time to read them and do any follow up for your collection.

CARD COMPANY AUCTIONS

Getting Started

Card companies long ago figured out they could find a collector to buy almost anything, so it would be difficult to convince them to turn over any items with memorabilia potential for free. But the card companies do conduct auctions, usually annually, to clean up shop. Items such as original artwork, photos, trial card lines that weren't financially successful, prototype cards, etc. are put up for sale to the highest bidder.

By their nature, participation in the card company auctions will cost you money, but you can limit the amount you spend. You'll want to steer clear of the more exotic, expensive items and concentrate on items that have unique appeal to your collection, but may be of little interest to other hobbyists.

Auctions are exciting. You never know what bargain you may find, what overlooked treasure you may uncover for your collection.

Steps

☐ Consult Appendix Y for a sample listing of the more common sports trading card company addresses.

☐ Select those companies whose products best suit your particular collection and write them a letter such as the one below, requesting information regarding whether they hold auctions, and if so when and where upcoming auctions are scheduled.

CARD COMPANY AUCTIONS (continued)

Card Company Name
Card Company Address

Attn: Public Relations Department

Dear Public Relations Department,

As a collector of select sports trading cards and other sports-related memorabilia, your products are important to my collection. Do you ever hold auctions of items either left over from or related to production runs?

Please send me any and all information related to auctions you may hold that include items that could be considered sports-related memorabilia. Please include information on upcoming date(s), time(s), and place(s) as well as sample listings of the types of items that may be available.

By the way, in the event I am unable to physically attend the auction, do you accept mail bids? If so, please enclose information regarding the proper procedure to participate.

Thank you for your prompt attention to my request. Enclosed is a stamped, self-addressed envelope for your response. I look forward to hearing from you soon.

Signed,

Your Name
Your Address

☐ Should auctions be held outside your local area, contact trading pals you may have in the area to see if they might attend for you. Give them specific written instructions regarding what to bid on and how much to bid. (This avoids potential misunderstandings.)

STORE PROMOTIONS

Getting Started

Find collectibles where you shop. At the beginning of the sports season or during major sporting events (i.e., Baseball's Annual All-Star Game) some companies offer free sports-related items with the purchase of their products. If the product is something you normally purchase anyway, then the free collectible is a super bonus. If you would not otherwise purchase the product, carefully weigh its cost versus the value of the free collectible.

Steps

☐ Pick up collectibles offered as promotional items when the free gift more than justifies the cost.

☐ Plan to take advantage of store promotions before they happen by obtaining a schedule of upcoming promotions. Contact corporate headquarters of major store chains (such as Safeway Stores) or major product producers (such as Kraft). Their addresses can be obtained through various sources, such as the local library or stock and bond brokerage houses. *Standard and Poor's Corporate Record* lists the addresses of corporations and is available in the reference section of many libraries. (Several sample company addresses are given in Appendix X.)

☐ Drop a note such as the following to corporations that interest you and whose products are locally availabe to you.

Some periodicals offer baseball cards as free inserts.

Companies often offer free memorabilia to consumers.

STORE PROMOTIONS
(continued)

Company Name
Company Address

Dear Company Marketing Department,

I collect sports memorabilia. Can you tell me if you have scheduled any professional sports-related promotions through your products? If so, when and where will they take place?

Enclosed is a self-addressed, stamped envelope for your response. Thank you for your assistance. I look forward to hearing from you soon.

Signed,

Your Name
Your Address

☐ Often life-size or other posters are featured in stores during a product promotion. When you spot one, contact the store manager. Ask when the promotion will be completed and whether you could pick up the poster at that time. Usually it would otherwise be thrown away. In courtesy to the store, make sure you show up punctually to pick up the collectible.

☐ MAKE LOOKING FOR SPORTS MEMORABILIA A PART OF YOUR WEEKLY SHOPPING!

RESTAURANT/EATERY PROMOTIONS

Getting Started

Fast food restaurants often team up with sports clubs to offer special promotions. Types of promotions can be as diverse as a cup with the team logo to an autograph session with a well-known player.

Here are several examples of company promotions we've recently experienced in our area. Baskin-Robbins served their ice cream sundaes in miniature collectible baseball batting helmets. You could ask to be served with your favorite team. 7-Eleven convenience stores offered plastic Slurpie cups sporting local team insignia with the purchase of a Slurpie.

Steps

The key is to be aware of what's happening in restaurants near you.

☐ Write directly to company headquarters of restaurants in your area using a letter such as the sample below. Ask for a schedule of upcoming promotions.

✉

Company Name
Company Address

Attn: Marketing/Promotions Department

Dear Company Marketing Department,

I collect sports memorabilia and frequent your restaurant often. Can you tell me what promotions you have scheduled for your restaurant this year using professional sports?

Please find enclosed a self-addressed, stamped envelope for your response. Thank you for your assistance. I look forward to hearing from you.

Signed,

Your Name
Your Address

✉

RESTAURANT/EATERY PROMOTIONS (continued)

☐ Write professional sports clubs in your area (see the Appendices for a variety of addresses, such as major league baseball, basketball, football, and ice hockey) at the beginning of the season requesting a list of promotions they have scheduled with different local restaurants.

✉

Team Name
Team Address

Attn: Team Public Relations Department

Dear Team Public Relations Department,

I am a longtime fan of your team and actively collect team memorabilia. Do you have any team promotions scheduled with local restaurants or other businesses?

Any information you could provide would be appreciated. A self-addressed, stamped envelope is enclosed for your response. Thank you for your assistance. I look forward to hearing from you soon. Good luck in the upcoming season!

Signed,

Your Name
Your Address

✉

RESTAURANT/EATERY PROMOTIONS (continued)

☐ Often unique posters and other memorabilia are featured in restaurants during promotions to increase customer awareness. When you spot one, contact the restaurant manager to find out what plans they have for these display items at the conclusion of the promotion. Frequently they will be thrown away and managers will happily let you take what they consider garbage off their hands at the appropriate time. But make sure you pick up the display items on a timely basis. Remember, in the manager's eyes, this is garbage. He's doing you a favor by saving it.

☐ Ask for more than one poster if available. Use it to trade with other collectors for desired memorabilia you would otherwise be unable to obtain.

MOVIE THEATERS

Getting Started

Almost every year at least one major movie featuring sports appears. Theaters usually advertise with posters.

If you contact theaters directly, you frequently can obtain the poster and other promotional material at no cost or for a minimal charge. In either case, you receive unique memorabilia for substantially less than if you were to try to obtain the same from a dealer or retail outlet.

Steps

☐ Refer to the telephone directory to identify movie theaters in your area.

☐ Call movie theater managers to request information regarding upcoming sports-related movies they may be aware of. Theaters learn about future movies to be released long in advance of advertisements to the public.

☐ Watch newspaper advertisements to identify movies that may be the topic of worthwhile memorabilia.

☐ While the movie is running in local theaters contact the theater managers to determine what they plan to do with the promotional materials after they are no longer needed. In many cases managers are quite willing to give them to you at the appropriate time instead of throwing them out. Pick materials up on time and the manager isn't inconvenienced at all. In this way, the manager often will express a willingness to continue to supply you with the theater's outdated promotional materials in the future.

RADIO/TELEVISION PROMOTIONS

Getting Started

Radio and television have been giving away free sports memorabilia to promote audience growth/loyalty for years. Most common is the call-in contest, which requires timing, persistence, and a bit of luck.

But a lot of stations who cover local teams in our area give away merchandise such as bumper stickers and team schedules as well. Usually all you have to do is visit the station or drop them a note to receive the free promotional merchandise.

Steps

☐ Consult your telephone directory for local radio and television station phone numbers.

☐ Contact them and ask if they have any promotions with professional sports teams planned in the near future.

☐ If you live in an area that doesn't have local professional sports teams, or are interested in sports memorabilia from teams outside your vicinity, try the following strategies.

Visit your local library to review out-of-area telephone directories to get the needed telephone numbers.

Write the team you desire memorabilia for (addresses for all professional baseball, basketball, football, and ice hockey teams can be found in the Appendices) and ask what promotions they have scheduled with television and radio stations. Then contact those stations regarding how you could obtain the promotional merchandise even though you live out of their area. Two sample letters follow.

RADIO/TELEVISION PROMOTIONS (continued)

✉

Team Name
Team Address

Attn: Team Public Relations Department

Dear Team Public Relations Department,

I am a longtime fan of your team and actively collect team memorabilia, but I live out of your area. What giveaway promotions do you have scheduled with radio and television stations local to you and that I might participate in? The type of promotion as well as name and address of the stations would be appreciated.

Any information you could provide would be appreciated. A self-addressed, stamped envelope is enclosed for your response.

Thank you for your assistance. I look forward to hearing from you. Good luck in the upcoming season!

Signed,

Your Name
Your Address

✉

Station Name
Station Address

Attn: Marketing/Promotions Manager

Dear Station Marketing Manager,

I collect sports memorabilia from (insert name of professional sports team here). Can you tell me how I might participate in any upcoming promotions you have scheduled?

I have enclosed a self-addressed, stamped envelope for your response. Thank you for your assistance. I look forward to hearing from you.

Signed,

Your Name
Your Address

✉

POST OFFICES

Getting Started

Post offices issue posters to promote newly-issued stamps. Once in awhile the topic is either a sport or a well-known former player. Much like store, restaurant, and movie promotions, you often can become the proud owner of these posters for little or no cost following the completion of the stamp's promotion.

For example, my wife is a stamp collector. Once when I accompanied her to the post office to pick up a new issue, I noticed a new Lou Gehrig stamp was being promoted with a great-looking poster. Just for asking, the postmaster allowed me to pick up the poster following the Lou Gehrig stamp's promotion. (You may even want to pick up a few of the actual stamps as well so you have a matched set.)

Steps

☐ Stamp collecting is called philately. Contact your local post office for the address and phone number of the United States Post Office Philately Division.

☐ Write the Philately Division a letter such as the following and ask for information on potential stamps to be issued involving sports.

POST OFFICES (continued)

U.S. Postal Service Philately Division
Address

Dear Philately Division,

I am especially interested in stamps that would be related to professional sports. Could you please inform me of any sports-related stamps you expect to issue in the upcoming year?

Any information you could supply would be appreciated. A self-addressed, stamped envelope is enclosed for your response.

Thank you for your attention to this request. I look forward to hearing from you soon.

Signed,

Your Name
Your Address

☐ Contact your local Postmaster regarding his willingness to pass on memorabilia used to promote these stamps to you after the post office is finished with it. Make sure you pick up the material promptly. It leaves a good impression and reinforces a good contact for future stamp promotional memorabilia.

GAS STATIONS

Getting Started

Gas stations have offered free or discounted sports items in exchange for your purchases for years. Since most of us need gas on a regular basis anyway, being an attentive gasoline purchaser can net unique sports memorabilia, especially with a regional focus.

Steps

☐ Be prepared. Be aware of promotions planned in your area. Visit gas stations of a cross section of companies in your area. Ask the owners what upcoming promotions they might be aware of that focus on sports.

☐ Ask local station owners or employees for the address of their company's headquarters. Write a letter such as the following to the marketing department in hopes of more detailed information.

✉

Company Name
Company Address

Attn: Marketing/Promotions Department

Dear Marketing Department,

I live in (insert your general geographic area here). I frequent your company's service station and am an avid collector of sports memorabilia. Any information you could provide regarding upcoming promotions I can expect through your stations would be appreciated.

Enclosed is a self-addressed, stamped envelope for your response. Thank you for your attention to my request. I look forward to hearing from you soon.

Signed,

Your Name
Your Address

✉

☐ You never know . . . Your letter may trigger the marketing department to begin thinking of sports promotions even if they didn't have any previously planned!

VIDEO SALES/ RENTAL STORES

Getting Started

Movies that were promoted once when they were released in theaters are promoted anew when their videos are released. Sometimes you are able to duplicate promotional memorabilia you obtained upon the film's initial release. Often you are able to get something entirely different just for asking.

Steps

☐ Look in the telephone directory to identify video sales/rental stores in your vicinity.

☐ Call store managers and ask about upcoming sports-related movies that recently were shown in theaters. Ask whether they are due to be re-released on video and when.

☐ Watch media advertisements, especially television, to identify sports-related movies that were blockbusters in theaters and are expected to be the same in video sales and rentals. They are good bets to be promoted with worthwhile memorabilia.

☐ Once the video has been released, ask video store managers what they plan to do with the promotional materials after they are no longer needed. In many cases managers are quite willing to give them to you at the appropriate time instead of throwing them out. Pick up materials on time and the manager isn't inconvenienced at all. In this way, the manager often will express a willingness to continue to supply you with the store's outdated promotional materials in the future.

BAKERY THRIFT STORES

Getting Started

At bakery thrift shops you can buy day-old bread, rolls, doughnuts, and other baked goods at reduced prices. In addition, for the reduced price you not only get the product, but also any promotional item that was originally offered with it. The result is more product and more memorabilia for less money.

Steps

☐ If the baked good was on your regular shopping list, it's like getting the promotional item for free.

☐ If you would not usually buy the baked good, but want the promotional sports item that comes with it, weigh the cost, even at its reduced level, against the value of the promotional item added to your collection. Given limited funds to expand your overall collection, you must decide which promotions warrant your participation.

PERSONAL COMPUTER SOFTWARE

Getting Started

A unique collectible that has yet to gain recognition is sports-related personal computer software. Baseball, basketball, hockey, and football games for the personal computer are often endorsed by well-known players. Sometimes a picture of the player is even featured on the box. For example, Pete Rose Pennant Fever has Pete's smiling face on the front. Imagine the worth unique items such as this could have ten or twenty years down the road.

Of course the key to true collectibles is limited supply. Personal computer software certainly fulfills this characteristic. With computer technology advancing as fast as it has, software often becomes quickly outdated. Products in any given form can only be purchased for a limited amount of time.

In addition, when a computer owner upgrades to a more advanced computer system, frequently the software used on the older model becomes incompatible and thus worthless. The computer owner has several choices: leave the software on the shelf collecting dust, try to sell it at a garage sale or flea market, or donate it to a local charity. All of these options require time and effort to plan and execute. By default, usually none of these options is selected and the software is simply thrown away. This means there will be a very limited amount of outdated software available to future collectors.

Collection of sports-related personal computer software as it goes out of date is a new frontier for sports-related memorabilia buffs. With a little effort you could be at the forefront.

Steps

☐ Visit computer software stores on a regular basis and make note of available sports-related software you think might have future collectible potential. ("Make note" is meant in the literal sense: actually write down the names of the programs and their manufacturer.)

PERSONAL COMPUTER SOFTWARE (continued)

☐ If your area has no comprehensive software stores, review recent copies of personal computer-oriented magazines. Skim for advertisements and articles that introduce sports-related software that might be of future interest to you. Again, make immediate note of program name and manufacturer.

☐ You don't have to subscribe to the magazines to get the information you need. Given the current popularity of personal computers, it is likely that someone you know already subscribes. Ask around. See if this someone will either lend or give you their back copies.

☐ When you notice the software is no longer available in stores, or when a major "upgrade" in the software is announced, it's time for the no cost/low cost collector to strike.

☐ Post flyers on public bulletin boards, such as at work, expressing your interest in outdated, sports-related personal computer software. If possible, list which programs in particular you are looking for. Don't specify what you are or are not willing to pay. Have interested parties call you for more information.

☐ While some owners might offer just to give you the outdated software they otherwise would have thrown out, most people are calling because they expect something in return. Negotiate a price that is beneficial to all.

☐ Personal computer magazines serve as more than a resource for current software with long-term collectible potential. Many of them have classified advertisement sections in the back. Often you can inexpensively place an ad expressing interest in sports-related software that no longer may be of use to its owner.

☐ It is highly recommended that you review several copies of a magazine to determine if it is likely to have the potential readership you are looking for, before you decide to run an ad.

Don't forget to ask stores for the box. They can have potentially valuable cards on the bottom, besides being memorabilia themselves.

DRUG AND CONVENIENCE STORES

Getting Started

In order to cater to customer needs, some drug, discount, and department stores now carry collections of sports trading cards. Most of these cards are sold in their traditional wax packs with so many packs to a box. Frequently the packs are bought in single units, not by box. Once the last pack is purchased the empty boxes are most often discarded by the stores.

Yet, for the savvy collector, these empty boxes are often collectibles in their own right. The box itself might carry a unique design or feature a star's picture. Many times the bottom and or sides of these boxes consist of collectible cards that are available nowhere else.

The store's garbage can enhance your collection.

Steps

☐ Find out which stores in your area carry cards as part of their regular stock.

☐ Ask store managers what they plan to do with empty boxes once all wax packs have been purchased.

☐ In many cases managers are quite willing to give them to you at the appropriate time instead of throwing them out.

☐ Schedule a regular time to come by and check for empty boxes. Pick the boxes up on time and the manager isn't inconvenienced at all. In this way, the manager often will be willing to continue to supply you with the store's empty trading card boxes.

☐ If you are in the market to buy trading cards, carry the packs you plan to purchase in the box up to the cash register and usually the sales clerk will let you leave the store with the box at no additional cost.

PUBLIC TRANSIT AUCTIONS

Getting Started

If you live in a large metropolitan area this is a surprisingly effective way to get low cost sports memorabilia. Often public transportation is used to get to and from games. Unfortunately for the transportation authority, fans discard items they no longer want by leaving them behind on trains, trams, and busses. The abandoned sports items end up in the transportation authority's lost and found department. Never claimed, they are auctioned off at regular intervals.

For example, in our area many fans use Bay Area Rapid Transit (BART) to attend Oakland Athletics games. At the most recent BART auction of unclaimed lost and found items, several A's batting helmets were auctioned off at prices substantially below retail.

Steps

☐ Consult your telephone directory for telephone numbers of local bus, taxi, and light-rail train authorities.

☐ Call your city and county government offices for the names and telephone numbers of other public transportation sources you may not have thought of.

☐ Contact the transportation authority's Lost and Found Department. Inquire about public auctions and ask to be added to their public auction mailing list.

☐ In return you should receive notice of upcoming auctions, their location, and even what will be available for sale.

ESTATE/GARAGE SALES

Getting Started

Garage and estate sales used to be a great place to find collectible treasures for cheap prices. Lately, however, many books have been written educating the public especially on how to maximize profit on garage sales. In addition, owners of sports memorabilia (especially sports trading cards) have become very savvy regarding their cards' value. This can make it tough to find garage sale bargains.

However, even if the prices aren't as cheap, you can still find one-of-a-kind memorabilia if you are patient and persistent. And while deals on trading cards may be few and far between, these same people may not be aware of the demand for other items you seek, such as game programs, pins, key chains, etc. You might find some pretty good deals.

Steps

☐ Watch your local newspaper for advertisements of upcoming estate and garage sales.

☐ To save wasted time, call those listed to check if sports memorabilia will be offered.

☐ Garage and estate sales can be demanding bartering sessions. Refresh your knowledge of memorabilia values before you go.

☐ Go early. Arrive before the crowd and while the widest variety of merchandise is available.

☐ Know what you are willing to pay and stick to it.

☐ Keep a pleasant manner in negotiations. You never know when you might find a new trading contact in the garage sale sponsor.

FLEA MARKETS

Getting Started

It's anyone's guess what you'll encounter at our nation's flea markets today. At least in our area, the vendors range from families looking to sell their discarded items to professional flea market vendors who make their livings from these informal gatherings. In recent years it has become common to find at each flea market at least one vendor specializing in sports-related memorabilia, especially trading cards. Watch out for high prices. These vendors know their wares.

The prices may not be as cheap as some other sources, but you can still find one-of-a-kind memorabilia if you are patient and persistent. And even if deals on trading cards may be few and far between, there are still less-informed vendors carrying a motley assortment of wares who may have hidden memorabilia treasures only a collector such as yourself would recognize. These items include old game programs, pins, key chains, old championship posters, T-shirts, etc. Take a relaxing walk around flea markets near you. Enjoy the fresh air and take your time. You never know, you might even find some pretty good deals.

Steps

☐ Watch your local newspaper for advertisements of upcoming flea markets.

☐ Visit the ones near you, not once, but several times. Vendors can vary from time to time. You'll need several trips to see if a particular flea market will have anything to offer.

☐ Flea markets offer challenging opportunities to barter. Refresh your knowledge of memorabilia values before you go.

☐ Go early, but stay awhile. Arrive before the crowd and while the widest variety of merchandise is available, but be aware some vendors aren't even set up for business until several hours after the flea market opens.

FLEA MARKETS (continued)

☐ Hang around the outskirts of a vendor's area that has some merchandise you may wish to bid on. Listen to how well he seems to know his wares and how flexible his prices are as he talks to other customers.

☐ Know what you're willing to pay and stick to it.

☐ Never forget the potential to trade merchandise you no longer want so that you can obtain desired memorabilia without paying cash.

CHARITIES/NON-PROFIT ORGANIZATIONS

Getting Started

Charities are big users of sports promotional material. For example, recently the United Way in our area used posters featuring San Francisco Giant Will Clark and Oakland Athletic Jose Canseco to promote annual local fundraising activities.

Steps

☐ Look in your telephone directory to identify charities in your area.

☐ Call your local city government offices and Chamber of Commerce for information about non-profit organizations they know of in your immediate vicinity.

☐ Contact the Secretary of State's Office in your state. Check with telephone information for the telephone number in your state's capital. The Secretary of State's Office usually maintains lists of all non-profit associations registered in the state. Their address can be obtained with a quick phone call to them. Make sure you ask if there is a charge for the list when you call. Some states do not provide the lists for free. In those cases, other alternatives for identifying charities may be preferable.

☐ Call charities you have identified and ask if they are using sports-related material to enhance their funding activities this year. When the answer is yes, you have several courses of action including:

Volunteer a certain portion of your time in exchange for the promotional items after the charity is finished with them.

Provide a small cash donation for the promotional items. This benefits everyone. You obtain desired and often unique memorabilia, while you help the charity meet their fund-raising objectives. In addition, you receive a tax deduction for your donation.

CHARITIES/NON-PROFIT ORGANIZATIONS (continued)

☐ Non-profit organizations also sometimes hold "games" with local celebrities against "old-timers," i.e., flag football or basketball, or with current players, as a fundraiser for charity, special cause. These present a great autograph opportunity, as well as the possibility of posters, flyers, and programs being given out. Perhaps raffle prizes at the event will include memorabilia — autographs, an old player uniform. Team Public Relations departments are a good source of information on what events are scheduled and which players will be participating. Also watch your local newspapers for these events.

☐ If you believe in the charity's cause, you may even wish to assist with the fundraiser. Consider buying a ticket to attend, or donate your time to help organize the event. You can maximize your autograph opportunity by requesting to help at dress rehearsal or practice, or better yet at the event itself. (You may want to write the player you wish an autograph from and say you are glad he is participating and you hope to see him there.)

COMMUNITY CENTERS

Getting Started

Community centers, as well as local parks and recreation departments, regularly try to put together programs that will benefit the local public. Frequently this includes at least annual trips to nearby professional sports events. To increase public awareness they create posters and other forms of announcements that could be handsome additions to your memorabilia collection.

In addition, once in awhile community centers will be the site of visits by local celebrities, who often include sports stars. What an opportunity this is for autographs and other memorabilia (as well as a chance to meet other interested collectors to trade with).

Steps

☐ Contact your local community center or parks and recreation department. Ask if they have any upcoming events scheduled for the public that are sports-related. Ask how these events will be promoted and what they plan to do with the promotional material after the event. Offer to take the material off their hands.

☐ Make sure you are added to the community center's and parks and recreation department's mailing lists so you are kept informed of upcoming activities.

POLICE ATHLETIC LEAGUES (PALS)

Getting Started

For both fundraising and public awareness tools, Police Athletic Leagues will often offer memorabilia such as special sports players trading cards, which carry a civic message in exchange for a small donation.

Steps

☐ Contact your local police department to see if they sponsor an Athletic League, then inquire whether they will be using any sports-related promotions in the coming year. You may wish to make a small donation so that you are added to their mailing list. Then announcements of upcoming promotions will be sent to you directly.

CITY GOVERNMENT

Getting Started

This technique is most effective when the local team is having a championship year. Proud of its sports celebrity, the city often tries to maximize the positive exposure by promoting the city featuring the sports team and/or players. Information about the city often includes sports memorabilia.

Steps

☐ Write a similar letter to the city government of your favorite team.

City Name
City Address

Dear City Name,

   I am interested in finding out more about your city and surrounding community. As an avid (insert name of sports team here) fan, I am especially interested in what role professional sports play in the quality of life in the area.

   Any information or promotional materials you could send would be appreciated. A self-addressed, stamped envelope is enclosed for your response. Thank you for your assistance. I look forward to hearing from you soon.

Signed,

Your Name
Your Address

CONTRARIAN STRATEGY

Getting Started

Buy low, sell high is the motto for more than successful stock market investing. Apply that advice to your sports memorabilia deals. Purchase sports memorabilia when it is out of season for lower prices. For example, during baseball season buy football memorabilia, during football season buy baseball memorabilia, etc.

Steps

☐ Avoid the urge to follow the crowd. Even though in summer your mind may be on your favorite baseball team, remember that other fans' minds will be too, so buy other sports' memorabilia, like ice hockey.

☐ In fact, if you are willing to spend a little, consider advertising to buy out-of-date merchandise right after a fall in its worth. For example: advertise to buy memorabilia of the local team right after it has lost the championship.

☐ In the same way, *never* buy at a sport's peak popularity period during its season, such as the football playoffs, the World Series, etc.

Part III
Collectors' Resources
Appendices

A: MAJOR LEAGUE BASEBALL ADDRESSES

American League

Baltimore Orioles
Memorial Stadium
Baltimore, MD 21218

Boston Red Sox
Fenway Park
24 Yawkey Way
Boston, MA 02215

California Angels
Anaheim Stadium
P.O. Box 2000
Anaheim, CA 92803

Chicago White Sox
Comiskey Park
324 West 35th Street
Chicago, IL 60616

Cleveland Indians
Cleveland Municipal Stadium
Cleveland, OH 44114-1098

Detroit Tigers
Tiger Stadium
Detroit, MI 48216

Kansas City Royals
Royal Stadium
P.O. Box 1969
Kansas City, MO 64141

Milwaukee Brewers
Milwaukee County Stadium
Milwaukee, WI 53214

Minnesota Twins
HHH Metrodome
501 Chicago Avenue South
Minneapolis, MN 55415

New York Yankees
Yankee Stadium
Bronx, NY 10451

Oakland Athletics
Oakland-Alameda Coliseum
Oakland, CA 94621

A: MAJOR LEAGUE BASEBALL ADDRESSES (continued)

Seattle Mariners
Kingdome
P.O. Box 4100
411 1st Avenue South
Seattle, WA 98104

Texas Rangers
Arlington Stadium
P.O. Box 1111
Arlington, TX 76004

Toronto Blue Jays
Skydome
300 The Esplanade West
Box 3200
Toronto, Ontario
Canada M5V 3B3

National League

Atlanta Braves
Atlanta-Fulton County Stadium
P.O. Box 4064
Atlanta, GA 30302

Chicago Cubs
Wrigley Field
1060 West Addison Street
Chicago, IL 60613

Cincinnati Reds
Riverfront Stadium
100 Riverfront Stadium
Cincinnati, OH 45202

Houston Astros
Astrodome
P.O. Box 288
Houston, TX 77001

Los Angeles Dodgers
Dodgers Stadium
1000 Elysian Park Avenue
Los Angeles, CA 90012

Montreal Expos
P.O. Box 500
Station M
Montreal, Quebec
Canada H1V 3P2

A: MAJOR LEAGUE BASEBALL ADDRESSES (continued)

New York Mets
Shea Stadium
Flushing, NY 11368

Philadelphia Phillies
Veterans Stadium
P.O. Box 7575
Philadelphia, PA 19101

Pittsburgh Pirates
Three Rivers Stadium
P.O. Box 7000
Pittsburgh, PA 15212

St. Louis Cardinals
Busch Memorial Stadium
250 Stadium Plaza
St. Louis, MO 63102

San Diego Padres
Jack Murphy Stadium
9449 Friars Road
San Diego, CA 92108

San Francisco Giants
Candlestick Park
San Francisco, CA 94124

B: MAJOR LEAGUE BASEBALL SPRING TRAINING ADDRESSES

American League

Baltimore Orioles
Miami Stadium
2301 NW 10th Avenue
Miami, FL 33127

Boston Red Sox
Chain O'Lakes Park
Cypress Gardens Blvd.
Winter Haven, FL 33880

California Angels
Angels Stadium
Sunrise Way & Baristo Road
Palm Springs, CA 92263

Chicago White Sox
Ed Smith Stadium
12th Street & Tuttle Avenue
Sarasota, FL 34237

Cleveland Indians
Hi Corbett Field
Randolph Park
Tucson, AZ 85726

Detroit Tigers
Joker Marchant Stadium
Al Kaline Drive
Lakeland Hills Blvd.
Lakeland, FL 33804

Kansas City Royals
Baseball City Stadium
Interstate 4 & US 27
P.O. Box 800
Orlando, FL 32802

Milwaukee Brewers
Compadre Stadium
1425 West Ocotillo Road
Chandler, AZ 85248

Minnesota Twins
Tinker Field
Tampa Avenue & Church Street
Orlando, FL 32855

B: MAJOR LEAGUE BASEBALL SPRING TRAINING ADDRESSES (continued)

New York Yankees
Ft. Lauderdale Stadium
5301 NW 12th Avenue
Ft. Lauderdale, FL 33309

Oakland Athletics
Phoenix Municipal Stadium
5999 East Van Buren
Phoenix, AZ 85008

Seattle Mariners
Tempe Diablo Stadium
2200 West Alameda
Tempe, AZ 85282

Texas Rangers
Charlotte County Stadium
2300 El Jobean Road
Port Charlotte, FL 33949

Toronto Blue Jays
Grant Field
311 Douglas Avenue
Dunedin, FL 34698

National League

Atlanta Braves
Municipal Stadium
715 Hank Aaron Drive
West Palm Beach, FL 33401

Chicago Cubs
Hohokam Park
1235 North Center Street
Mesa, AZ 85201

Cincinnati Reds
Plant City Stadium
1900 South Park Road
Plant City, FL 34289

Houston Astros
Osceola County Stadium
1000 Osceola Blvd.
Kissimmee, FL 32741

B: MAJOR LEAGUE BASEBALL SPRING TRAINING ADDRESSES (continued)

Los Angeles Dodgers
Holman Stadium
40001 26th Street
Vero Beach, FL 32961

Montreal Expos
Municipal Stadium
715 Hank Aaron Drive
West Palm Beach, FL 33401

New York Mets
St. Lucie County Sports Complex
525 NW Peacock Blvd.
Port St. Lucie, FL 34986

Philadelphia Phillies
Jack Russell Stadium
800 Phillies Drive
Clearwater, FL 34617

Pittsburgh Pirates
McKechnie Field
17th Avenue & 9th Street West
Bradenton, FL 34208

St. Louis Cardinals
Al Lang Stadium
180 2nd Avenue SE
St. Petersburg, FL 33701

San Diego Padres
Desert Sun Stadium
1440 Desert Sun Stadium
Avenue A at 35th Street
Yuma, AZ 85364

San Francisco Giants
Scottsdale Stadium
7408 East Osborne Road
Scottsdale, AZ 85251

C: TRIPLE-A MINOR LEAGUE BASEBALL ADDRESSES

American Association

Buffalo Bisons
Pittsburgh Pirates
P.O. Box 450
Buffalo, NY 14205

Denver Zephyrs
Milwaukee Brewers
2850 West 20th Street
Denver, CO 80211

Indianapolis Indians
Montreal Expos
1501 West 16th Street
Indianapolis, IN 46202

Iowa Cubs
Chicago Cubs
2nd and Riverside Drive
Des Moines, IA 50309

Louisville Redbirds
St. Louis Cardinals
P.O. Box 36407
Louisville, KY 40233

Nashville Sounds
Cincinatti Reds
P.O. Box 23290
Nashville, TN 37202

Oklahoma City 89ers
Texas Rangers
P.O. Box 75089
Oklahoma, OK 73147

Omaha Royals
Kansas City Royals
P.O. Box 3665
Omaha, NE 68103

International League

Columbus Clippers
New York Yankees
1155 West Mount Street
Columbus, OH 43223

C: TRIPLE-A MINOR LEAGUE BASEBALL ADDRESSES (continued)

Pawtucket Red Sox
Boston Red Sox
P.O. Box 2365
Pawtucket, RI 02861

Richmond Braves
Atlanta Braves
P.O. Box 6667
Richmond, VA 23230

Rochester Red Wings
Baltimore Orioles
500 Norton Street
Rochester, NY 14621

Scranton/Wilkes-Barre Red Barons
Philadelphia Phillies
P.O. Box 3449
Scranton, PA 18505

Syracuse Chiefs
Toronto Blue Jays
MacArthur Stadium
Syracuse, NY 13208

Tidewater Tides
New York Mets
P.O. Box 12111
Norfolk, VA 23502

Toledo Mud Hens
Detroit Tigers
P.O. Box 6212
Toledo, OH 43614

Pacific Coast League

Albuquerque Dukes
Los Angeles Dodgers
P.O. Box 26267
Albuquerque, NM 87125

Calgary Cannons
Seattle Mariners
P.O. Box 3690
Station B
Calgary, Alberta
Canada T2M 4M4

C: TRIPLE-A MINOR LEAGUE BASEBALL ADDRESSES (continued)

Colorado Springs Sky Sox
Cleveland Indians
4385 Tutt Avenue
Colorado Springs, CO 80922

Edmonton Trappers
California Angels
10233 96th Avenue
Edmonton, Alberta
Canada T5K 0A5

Las Vegas Stars
San Diego Padres
850 Las Vegas Blvd. North
Las Vegas, NV 89101

Phoenix Firebirds
San Francisco Giants
5999 East Van Buren Street
Phoenix, AZ 85008

Portland Beavers
Minnesota Twins
P.O. Box 1659
Portland, OR 97207

Tacoma Tigers
Oakland Athletics
P.O. Box 11087
Tacoma, WA 98411

Tucson Toros
Houston Astros
P.O. Box 27045
Tucson, AZ 85726

Vancouver Canadians
Chicago White Sox
4601 Ontario Street
Vancouver, British Columbia
Canada V5V 3H4

D: DOUBLE-A MINOR LEAGUE BASEBALL ADDRESSES

Eastern League

Albany-Colonie Yankees
New York Yankees
Albany-Shaker Road
Albany, NY 12211

Canton-Akron Indians
Cleveland Indians
Canton, OH 44707

Hagerstown Suns
Baltimore Orioles
P.O. Box 230
Hagerstown, MD 21741

Harrisburg Senators
Pittsburgh Pirates
P.O. Box 15757
Harrisburg, PA 17105

London Tigers
Detroit Tigers
89 Wharncliffe Road North
London, Ontario
Canada N6H 2A7

New Britain Red Sox
Boston Red Sox
P.O. Box 1718
New Britain, CT 06050

Reading Phillies
Philadelphia Phillies
P.O. Box 15050
Reading, PA 19612

Williamsport Bills
Seattle Mariners
P.O. Box 474
Williamsport, PA 17703

Southern League

Birmingham Barons
Chicago White Sox
P.O. Box 360007
Birmingham, AL 35236

D: DOUBLE-A MINOR LEAGUE BASEBALL ADDRESSES (continued)

Charlotte Knights
Chicago Cubs
2280 Deerfield Drive
Fort Mill, SC 29715

Chattanooga Lookouts
Cincinnati Reds
P.O. Box 11002
Chattanooga, TN 37401

Columbus Mudcats
Houston Astros
P.O. Box 2425
Columbus, GA 31902

Greenville Braves
Atlanta Braves
P.O. Box 16683
Greenville, SC 29606

Huntsville Stars
Oakland Athletics
P.O. Box 14099
Huntsville, AL 35815

Jacksonville Expos
Montreal Expos
P.O. Box 4756
Jacksonville, FL 32201

Knoxville Blue Jays
Toronto Blue Jays
633 Jessamine Street
Knoxville, TN 37917

Memphis Chicks
Kansas City Royals
800 Home Run Lane
Memphis, TN 38104

Orlando Twins
Minnesota Twins
P.O. Box 5645
Orlando, FL 32855

D: DOUBLE-A MINOR LEAGUE BASEBALL ADDRESSES (continued)

Texas League

Arkansas Travelers
St. Louis Cardinals
P.O. Box 5599
Little Rock, AR 72215

El Paso Diablos
Milwaukee Brewers
P.O. Box 9337
El Paso, TX 79984

Jackson Mets
New York Mets
P.O. Box 4209
Jackson, MS 39296

Midland Angels
California Angels
P.O. Box 12
Midland, TX 79702

San Antonio Missions
Los Angeles Dodgers
P.O. Box 28268
San Antonio, TX 78228

Shreveport Captains
San Francisco Giants
P.O. Box 3448
Shreveport, LA 71133

Tulsa Drillers
Texas Rangers
P.O. Box 4448
Tulsa, OK 74159

Wichita Wranglers
San Diego Padres
P.O. Box 1420
Wichita, KS 67201

E: SINGLE-A MINOR LEAGUE BASEBALL ADDRESSES

California League

Bakersfield Dodgers
Los Angeles Dodgers
P.O. Box 10031
Bakersfield, CA 93389

Modesto A'S
Oakland Athletics
P.O. Box 2437
Modesto, CA 95351

Palm Springs Angels
California Angels
P.O. Box 1742
Palm Springs, CA 92263

Reno Silver Sox
Independent
P.O. Box 11363
Reno, NV 89510

Riverside Red Wave
San Diego Padres
P.O. Box 5487
Riverside, CA 92517

Salinas Spurs
Co-op
P.O. Box 4370
Salinas, CA 93912

San Bernardino Spirit
Seattle Mariners
P.O. Box 30160
San Bernardino, CA 92143

San Jose Giants
San Francisco Giants
P.O. Box 21727
San Jose, CA 95151

Stockton Ports
Milwaukee Brewers
Sutter and Alpine
Stockton, CA 95204

Visalia Oaks
Minnesota Twins
P.O. Box 48
Visalia, CA 93279

E: SINGLE-A MINOR LEAGUE BASEBALL ADDRESSES (continued)

Carolina League

Durham Bulls
Atlanta Braves
P.O. Box 507
Durham, NC 27702

Frederick Keys
Baltimore Orioles
P.O. Box 3169
Frederick, MD 21701

Kinston Indians
Cleveland Indians
P.O. Box 3542
Kinston, NC 28502

Lynchburg Red Sox
Boston Red Sox
P.O. Box 10213
Lynchburg, VA 24506

Peninsula Pilots
Co-op
P.O. Box 9194
Hampton, VA 23670

Prince William Cannons
New York Yankees
P.O. Box 2148
Woodbridge, VA 22193

Salem Buccaneers
Pittsburgh Pirates
P.O. Box 842
Salem, VA 24153

Winston-Salem Spirits
Chicago Cubs
P.O. Box 4488
Winston-Salem, NC 27115

Florida State League

Baseball City Royals
Kansas City Royals
P.O. Box 800
Orlando, FL 32802

E: SINGLE-A MINOR LEAGUE BASEBALL ADDRESSES (continued)

Charlotte Rangers
Texas Rangers
P.O. Box 3609
Port Charlotte, FL 33949

Clearwater Phillies
Philadelphia Phillies
P.O. Box 10336
Clearwater, FL 34617

Dunedin Blue Jays
Toronto Blue Jays
P.O. Box 957
Dunedin, FL 34697

Fort Lauderdale Yankees
New York Yankees
5301 NW 12th Street
Fort Lauderdale, FL 33309

Lakeland Tigers
Detroit Tigers
P.O. Box 2785
Lakeland, FL 33806

Miami Miracle
Independent
7875 NW 12th Street
Miami, FL 33126

Osceola Astros
Houston Astros
P.O. Box 2229
Kissimmee, FL 32742

St. Lucie Mets
New York Mets
P.O. Box 8808
Port St. Lucie, FL 34985

St. Petersburg Cardinals
St. Louis Cardinals
P.O. Box 12557
St. Petersburg, FL 33733

Sarasota White Sox
Chicago White Sox
P.O. Box 9
Sarasota, FL 34230

E: SINGLE-A MINOR LEAGUE BASEBALL ADDRESSES (continued)

Vero Beach Dodgers
Los Angeles Dodgers
P.O. Box 2887
Vero Beach, FL 32961

West Palm Beach Expos
Montreal Expos
P.O. Box 3566
West Palm Beach, FL 33402

Winter Haven Red Sox
Boston Red Sox
Winter Haven, FL 33880

Midwest League

Appleton Foxes
Kansas City Royals
P.O. Box 464
Appleton, WI 54912

Beloit Brewers
Milwaukee Brewers
P.O. Box 855
Beloit, WI 53511

Burlington Braves
Atlanta Braves
P.O. Box 824
Burlington, IA 52601

Cedar Rapids Reds
Cincinnati Reds
P.O. Box 2001
Cedar Rapids, IA 52406

Clinton Giants
San Francisco Giants
P.O. Box 789
Clinton, IA 52732

Kenosha Twins
Minnesota Twins
P.O. Box 661
Kenosha, WI 53141

E: SINGLE-A MINOR LEAGUE BASEBALL ADDRESSES (continued)

Madison Muskies
Oakland Athletics
P.O. Box 882
Madison, WI 53701

Peoria Chiefs
Chicago Cubs
1524 West Nebraska Avenue
Peoria, IL 61604

Quad City Angels
California Angels
P.O. Box 3496
Davenport, IA 52808

Rockford Expos
Montreal Expos
P.O. Box 6748
Rockford, IL 61125

South Bend White Sox
Chicago White Sox
P.O. Box 4218
South Bend, IN 46634

Springfield Cardinals
St. Louis Cardinals
P.O. Box 3004
Springfield, IL 62708

Waterloo Diamonds
Co-op
P.O. Box 611
Waterloo, IA 50704

Wausau Timbers
Seattle Mariners
P.O. Box 1704
Wausau, WI 54402

South Atlantic League

Asheville Tourists
Houston Astros
P.O. Box 1556
Asheville, NC 28802

E: SINGLE-A MINOR LEAGUE BASEBALL ADDRESSES (continued)

Augusta Pirates
Pittsburgh Pirates
P.O. Box 3746-Hill Station
Augusta, GA 30904

Charleston (SC) Rainbows
San Diego Padres
P.O. Box 2840
Charleston, SC 29403

Charleston (WV) Wheelers
Chicago Cubs
P.O. Box 2669
Charleston, WV 25304

Columbia Mets
New York Mets
P.O. Box 7845
Columbia, SC 29202

Fayetteville Generals
Detroit Tigers
P.O. Box 64939
Fayetteville, NC 28306

Gastonia Rangers
Texas Rangers
P.O. Box 309
Gastonia, NC 28053

Greensboro Hornets
Cincinnati Reds
P.O. Box 22093
Greensboro, NC 27420

Myrtle Beach Blue Jays
Toronto Blue Jays
P.O. Box 1110
Myrtle Beach, SC 29578

Savannah Cardinals
St. Louis Cardinals
P.O. Box 3783
Savannah, GA 31414

Spartanburg Phillies
Philadelphia Phillies
P.O. Box 1721
Spartanburg, SC 29304

E: SINGLE-A MINOR LEAGUE BASEBALL ADDRESSES (continued)

Sumter Braves
Atlanta Braves
P.O. Box 2878
Sumter, SC 29151

New York-Penn League

Auburn Astros
Houston Astros
P.O. Box 651
Auburn, NY 13021

Batavia Clippers
Philadelphia Phillies
P.O. Box 802
Batavia, NY 14021

Elmira Pioneers
Boston Red Sox
P.O. Box 238
Elmira, NY 14902

Erie Orioles
Baltimore Orioles
P.O. Box 488
Erie, PA 16512

Geneva Cubs
Chicago Cubs
P.O. Box 402
Geneva, NY 14456

Hamilton Redbirds
St. Louis Cardinals
P.O. Box 1200, Station A
Hamilton, Ontario
Canada L8N 4B4

Jamestown Expos
Montreal Expos
P.O. Box 338
Jamestown, NY 14701

Niagara Falls Rapids
Detroit Tigers
1201 Hyde Park Blvd.
Niagara Falls, NY 14305

E: SINGLE-A MINOR LEAGUE BASEBALL ADDRESSES (continued)

Oneonta Yankees
New York Yankees
95 River Street
Oneonta, NY 13820

Pittsfield Mets
New York Mets
P.O. Box 328
Pittsfield, MA 01202

St. Catharines Blue Jays
Toronto Blue Jays
P.O. Box 1088
St. Catharines, Ontario
Canada L2R 3B0

Utica Blue Sox
Chicago White Sox
P.O. Box 751
Utica, NY 13503

Watertown Indians
Cleveland Indians
P.O. Box 802
Watertown, NY 13601

Welland Pirates
Pittsburgh Pirates
P.O. Box 594
Welland, Ontario
Canada L3B 5R3

Northwest League

Bellingham Mariners
Seattle Mariners
1500 Orleans Street
Bellingham, WA 98226

Bend Bucks
California Angels
Bend, OR 97708

Boise Hawks
Independent
1109 Main Street, Suite C
Boise, ID 83702

E: SINGLE-A MINOR LEAGUE BASEBALL ADDRESSES (continued)

Eugene Emeralds
Kansas City Royals
P.O. Box 5566
Eugene, OR 97405

Everett Giants
San Francisco Giants
P.O. Box 1346
Everett, WA 98206

Salem Dodgers
Los Angeles Dodgers
P.O. Box 17641
Salem, OR 97305

Southern Oregon Athletics
Oakland Athletics
P.O. Box 1457
Medford, OR 97501

Spokane Indians
San Diego Padres
P.O. Box 4758
Spokane, WA 99202

Appalachian League

Bluefield Orioles
Baltimore Indians
P.O. Box 356
Bluefield, WV 24701

Bristol Tigers
Detroit Tigers
P.O. Box 1434
Bristol, VA 24203

Burlington Indians
Cleveland Indians
P.O. Box 1143
Burlington, NC 27216

Elizabethton Twins
Minnesota Twins
P.O. Box 6040
Elizabethton, TN 37644

E: SINGLE-A MINOR LEAGUE BASEBALL ADDRESSES (continued)

Johnson City Cardinals
St. Louis Cardinals
P.O. Box 568
Johnson City, TN 37601

Kingsport Mets
New York Mets
P.O. Box 3522
Kingsport, TN 37664

Martinsville Phillies
Philadelphia Phillies
P.O. Box 3614
Martinsville, VA 24115

Princeton Pirates
Pittsburgh Pirates
Municipal Building
Princeton, WV 24720

Pulaski Braves
Atlanta Braves
P.O. Box 814
Pulaski, VA 24301

Wytheville Cubs
Chicago Cubs
P.O. Box 972
Wytheville, VA 24382

Pioneer League

Billings Mustangs
Cincinnati Reds
P.O. Box 1553
Billings, MT 59103

Butte Copper Kings
Texas Rangers
P.O. Box 186
Butte, MT 59703

Great Falls Dodgers
Los Angeles Dodgers
P.O. Box 1621
Great Falls, MT 59403

E: SINGLE-A MINOR LEAGUE BASEBALL ADDRESSES (continued)

Helena Brewers
Milwaukee Brewers
P.O. Box 4606
Helena, MT 59604

Idaho Falls Braves
Atlanta Braves
P.O. Box 2183
Idaho Falls, ID 83403

Medicine Hat Blue Jays
Toronto Blue Jays
P.O. Box 465
Medicine Hat, Alberta
Canada T1A 0A5

Pocatello Giants
San Francisco Giants
P.O. Box 4668
Pocatello, ID 83205

Salt Lake Trappers
Independent
1325 South Main #102
Salt Lake City, UT 84115

F: NATIONAL BASKETBALL ASSOCIATION ADDRESSES

Atlanta Hawks
100 Techwood Drive NW
Atlanta, GA 30303

Boston Celtics
150 Causeway Street
Boston, MA 02114

Charlotte Hornets
Two First Union Plaza
Suite 2600
Charlotte, NC 28282

Chicago Bulls
One Magnificent Mile
980 North Michigan Avenue
Suite 1600
Chicago, IL 60611

Cleveland Cavaliers
P.O. Box 5000
Richfield, OH 44286-5000

Dallas Mavericks
Reunion Arena
777 Sports Street
Dallas, TX 75207

Denver Nuggets
P.O. Box 4658
Denver, CO 80204-6700

Detroit Pistons
The Palace of Auburn Hills
3777 Lapeer Road
Auburn Hills, MI 48057

Golden State Warriors
Oakland Coliseum Arena
Nimitz Freeway & Hegenberger Road
Oakland, CA 94621

Houston Rockets
P.O. Box 272349
Houston, TX 77277

Indiana Pacers
Two West Washington
Suite 510
Indianapolis, IN 46204

F: NATIONAL BASKETBALL ASSOCIATION ADDRESSES (continued)

Los Angeles Clippers
Los Angeles Sports Stadium
3939 South Figueroa
Los Angeles, CA 90306

Los Angeles Lakers
P.O. Box 10
Inglewood, CA 90306

Miami Heat
Miami Arena
Miami, FL 33136-4102

Milwaukee Bucks
901 North Fourth Street
Milwaukee, WI 53203

Minnesota Timberwolves
730 Hennepin Avenue
Suite 500
Minneapolis, MN 55403

New Jersey Nets
Brendan Byrne Arena
East Rutherford, NJ 07073

New York Knicks
4 Pennsylvania Plaza
New York, NY 10001

Orlando Magic
1 Dupont Center
390 North Orange Avenue
Suite 275
Orlando, FL 32801

Philadelphia 76ers
Veterans Stadium
P.O. Box 25040
Philadelphia, PA 19147

Phoenix Suns
P.O. Box 1369
Phoenix, AZ 85001

Portland Trail Blazers
700 NE Multnomah Street
Suite 950, Lloyd Building
Portland, OR 97232

F: NATIONAL BASKETBALL ASSOCIATION ADDRESSES (continued)

Sacramento Kings
1515 Sports Drive
Sacramento, CA 95834

San Antonio Spurs
600 East Market
Suite 102
San Antonio, TX 78205

Seattle Supersonics
Box C-900911
Seattle, WA 98109-9711

Utah Jazz
5 Triad Center
5th Floor
Salt Lake City, UT 84180

Washington Bullets
Capital Center
One Harry S Truman Drive
Landover, MD 20785

G: CONTINENTAL BASKETBALL ASSOCIATION ADDRESSES

Albany Patrons
112 State Street
Suite 1114
Albany, NY 12207

Cedar Rapids Silver Bullets
117 First Avenue SE
Cedar Rapids, IA 52401

Columbus Horizon
632 East 11th Street
Columbus, OH 43211

Grand Rapids Hoops
124 Lyon NW
Grand Rapids, MI 49503

La Crosse Catbirds
312 State Street
La Crosse, WI 54601

Oklahoma City Cavalry
1 Myriad Gardens
Oklahoma City, OK 73102

Omaha Racers
63rd & Shirley
Omaha, NE 68106

Pensacola Tornados
P.O. Box 12421
Pensacola, FL 32382-2421

Quad City Thunder
329 18th Street
Rock Island, IL 61201

Rapid City Thrillers
444 Mt. Rushmore Road North
Rapid City, SD 57701

Rockford Lightning
404 Elm Street
Rockford, IL 61101

San Jose Jammers
3487 McKee Road #55
San Jose, CA 95127

G: CONTINENTAL BASKETBALL ASSOCIATION ADDRESSES (continued)

Sioux Falls Skyforce
330 North Main Avenue #101
Sioux Falls, SD 57102

Tulsa Fast Breakers
5970 East 31st
Suite M
Tulsa, OK 74135

Wichita Falls Texans
2304 Midwestern Pkwy. #200
Wichita Falls, TX 76308

Yakima Sun Kings
609 East Yakima Avenue
Yakima, WA 98901

H: WORLD BASKETBALL LEAGUE ADDRESSES

Calgary 88's
205 9th Avenue SE
Suite 503
Calgary, Alberta
Canada T2G 0R3

Las Vegas Silver Streak
4634 S. Maryland Pkwy.
Suite 109
Las Vegas, NV 89119

Illinois Express
619 East Monroe Street
Suite 200
Springfield, IL 62701

Worcester Counts
50 Foster Street
P.O. Box 2533
Worcester, MA 01608

Youngstown Pride
20 Federal Plaza West
P.O. Box 987
Phar-Mor Center
Youngstown, OH 44501

I: NATIONAL FOOTBALL LEAGUE ADDRESSES

Atlanta Falcons
Suwanee Road at I-85
Suwanee, GA 30174

Buffalo Bills
One Bills Drive
Orchard Park, NY 14127

Chicago Bears
250 North Washington Road
Lake Forest, IL 60045

Cincinnati Bengals
200 Riverfront Stadium
Cincinnati, OH 45202

Cleveland Browns
Tower B
Cleveland Stadium
Cleveland, OH 44114

Dallas Cowboys
One Cowboys Parkway
Irving, TX 75063

Denver Broncos
13655 East Dove Valley Parkway
Englewood, CO 80112

Detroit Lions
1200 Featherstone Road
Pontiac, MI 48057

Green Bay Packers
1265 Lombardi Avenue
Green Bay, WI 54303

Houston Oilers
6910 Fannin Street
Houston, TX 77030

Indianapolis Colts
7001 West 56th Street
Indianapolis, IN 46254

Kansas City Chiefs
One Arrowhead Drive
Kansas City, MO 64129

I: NATIONAL FOOTBALL LEAGUE ADDRESSES (continued)

Los Angeles Raiders
332 Center Street
El Segundo, CA 90245

Los Angeles Rams
2327 West Lincoln Avenue
Anaheim, CA 92801

Miami Dolphins
Joe Robbie Stadium
2269 NW 199th Street

Miami, FL 33117
Minnesota Vikings
9520 Viking Drive
Eden Prairie, MN 55334

New England Patriots
Sullivan Stadium, Route 1
Foxboro, MA 02035

New Orleans Saints
1500 Poydras Street
New Orleans, LA 70112

New York Giants
Giants Stadium
East Rutherford, NJ 07073

New York Jets
598 Madison Avenue
New York, NY 10022

Philadelphia Eagles
Veterans Stadium
Broad Street and Pattison Avenue
Philadelphia, PA 19148

Phoenix Cardinals
P.O. Box 888
Phoenix, AZ 85001-0888

Pittsburgh Steelers
300 Stadium Circle
Pittsburgh, PA 15212

I: NATIONAL FOOTBALL LEAGUE ADDRESSES (continued)

San Diego Chargers
Jack Murphy Stadium
P.O. Box 20666
San Diego, CA 92120

San Francisco Forty-Niners
4949 Centennial Blvd.
Santa Clara, CA 95054

Seattle Seahawks
11220 NE 53rd Street
Kirkland, WA 98033

Tampa Bay Buccaneers
One Buccaneer Place
Tampa, FL 33607

Washington Redskins
P.O. Box 17247
Dulles International Airport
Washington, DC 20041

J: MINOR LEAGUE FOOTBALL ADDRESSES

Bay State Titans
1 City Hall Square
Lynn, MA 01901

California Outlaws
1779 Tribute Road
Sacramento, CA 95815

Charlotte Barons
1101 Clawson Court
P.O. Box 12243
Charlotte, NC 28220

Colorado Springs Spirit
532 Garden of the Gods Road
Colorado Springs, CO 80907

Florida Renegades
3944 Florida Blvd.
Palm Beach Gardens, FL 33410

Fresno Bandits
2300 Tulare Street
Fresno, CA 93721

Harrisburg Patriots
401 North 6th Street
Harrisburg, PA 17108

Middle Georgia Heatwave
964 Georgia Avenue
Macon, GA 31201

Oklahoma City Twisters
2616 South I-35
Oklahoma, OK 73129

Pueblo Crusaders
301 North Main Street
Pueblo, CO 81003

Scranton/Wilkes-Barre
129 N. Washington Avenue
Scranton, PA 18503

Tacoma Express
2501 East D Street
Tacoma, WA 98421

K: CANADIAN FOOTBALL LEAGUE ADDRESSES

British Columbia Lions
10605 135th Street
British Columbia
Canada V3T 4C8

Calgary Stampeders
McMahon Stadium
1827 Crowchild Trail NW
Calgary, Alberta
Canada T2M 4T6

Edmonton Eskimos
9023-111 Avenue
Edmonton, Alberta
Canada T5B 0X3

Hamilton Tiger-Cats
75 Balsam Avenue North
Hamilton, Ontario
Canada L8N 3A2

Montreal Alouettes
P.O. Box 100
Station M
Montreal, Quebec
Canada H1V 3L6

Ottawa Roughriders
Lansdowne Park
Ottawa, Ontario
Canada K1S 3W7

Saskatchewan Roughrider
2940 10th Avenue
Regina, Saskatchewan
Canada S4P 3B8

Toronto Argonauts
Exhibition Stadium
Toronto, Ontario
Canada M6K 3C3

Winnipeg Blue Bombers
1465 Maroons Road
Winnipeg, Manitoba
Canada R3G 0L6

L: SEMI-PRO FOOTBALL ADDRESSES

Arena Football League
2250 East Devon Avenue
#337
Des Plaines, IL 60018

Continental Interstate Football League
12 Kenneth Drive
Walkersville, MD 21793

Eastern Football League
55 Brookside Drive
Winchester, MA 01890

Empire Football League
53 James Street
Hudson, NY 12534

M: NATIONAL HOCKEY LEAGUE ADDRESSES

Boston Bruins
Boston Garden
150 Causeway Street
Boston, MA 02114

Buffalo Sabres
Memorial Auditorium
Buffalo, NY 14202

Calgary Flames
The Olympic Saddledome
P.O. Box 1540
Station M
Calgary, Alberta
Canada T2P 3B9

Chicago Black Hawks
Chicago Stadium
1800 West Madison Street
Chicago, IL 60612

Detroit Red Wings
Joe Louis Sports Arena
600 Civic Drive
Detroit, MI 48226

Edmonton Oilers
7424 118th Avenue
Edmonton, Alberta
Canada T5B 4M9

Hartford Whalers
Hartford Civic Center
One Civic Center Plaza
Hartford, CT 06103

Los Angeles Kings
The Forum
P.O. Box 10
Inglewood, CA 90306

Minnesota North Stars
Metropolitan Sports Center
7901 Cedar Avenue South
Bloomington, MN 55420

Montreal Canadiens
Montreal Forum
2313 St. Catherine Street West
Montreal, Quebec
Canada H3H 1N2

M: NATIONAL HOCKEY LEAGUE ADDRESSES (continued)

New Jersey Devils
Byrne Meadowland Sports Center
P.O. Box 504
East Rutherford, NJ 07073

New York Islanders
Nassau Veterans Memorial Coliseum
Uniondale, NY 11553

New York Rangers
Madison Square Garden
4 Pennsylvania Plaza
New York, NY 10001

Philadelphia Flyers
The Spectrum
Pattison Place
Philadelphia, PA 19148

Pittsburgh Penguins
Civic Arena
Gate No. 7
Pittsburgh, PA 15219

Quebec Nordiques
2205 Avenue du Colisee
Quebec City, Quebec
Canada G1L 4W7

St. Louis Blues
The Arena
5700 Oakland Avenue
St. Louis, MO 63110

Toronto Maple Leafs
Maple Leaf Gardens
60 Carlton Street
Toronto, Ontario
Canada M6B 1L1

Vancouver Canucks
Pacific Coliseum
100 North Renfrew Street
Vancouver, British Columbia
Canada V5K 3N7

Washington Capitals
Capital Centre
Landover, MD 20786

M: NATIONAL HOCKEY LEAGUE ADDRESSES (continued)

Winnipeg Jets
Winnipeg Arena
15-1430 Maroons Road
Winnipeg, Manitoba
Canada R3G 0L5

N: SEMI-PRO HOCKEY ADDRESSES

American Hockey League
425 Union Street
West Springfield, MA 01089

International Hockey League
3850 Priority Way South Drive
Suite 104
Indianapolis, IN 46240

O: WORLD SOCCER LEAGUE ADDRESSES

Arizona Condors
4210 N. Brown Avenue
Suite B
Scottsdale, AZ 85251

California Kickers
3473 Moore Street
Los Angeles, CA 90066

Los Angeles Heat
220 South Pacific Coast Hwy.
Suite 104
Redondo Beach, CA 90277

Portland Timbers
10725 SW Barbur Blvd.
Suite 390
Portland, OR 97219

Real Santa Barbara
105 East De La Guerra
Suite 4
Santa Barbara, CA 93101

Sacramento Senators
5560 Palm Avenue
Suite C
Sacramento, CA 95841

San Diego Nomads
1298 Prospect Street
La Jolla, CA 92037

San Francisco Bay Blackhawks
3820 Blackhawk Road
Danville, CA 94526

Seattle Storm
2815 Second Avenue
Suite 590
Seattle, WA 98121

P: CANADIAN SOCCER LEAGUE ADDRESSES

Calgary Strikers
5115 Crowchild Trail SW
Calgary, Alberta
Canada T3E 1T9

Edmonton Brick Men
10233 96th Avenue
Edmonton, Alberta
Canada T5K 0A5

Hamilton Steelers
One James Street South
10th Floor
Hamilton, Ontario
Canada L8P 4R5

Montreal Supra
C.P. 3028 Station Youville
Montreal, Quebec
Canada H2P 2Y8

North York Rockets
2250 Queen Street East
Brampton, Ontario
Canada L6T 3S1

Ottawa Intrepid
P.O. Box 2025, Station D
340 Laurier Avenue West
Ottawa, Ontario
Canada K1P 5W3

Toronto Blizzard
5310 Explorer Drive
Mississauga, Ontario
Canada L4W 4J6

Vancouver 86ers
6255 McKay Avenue
Burnaby, British Columbia
Canada V5H 2W7

Victoria Vistas
1312 Blanshard Street
Suite 301
Victoria, British Columbia
Canada V8W 3K5

Winnipeg Fury
1670 Portage Avenue
Winnipeg, Manitoba
Canada R3J 0C9

Q: LEAGUE OFFICE ADDRESSES

Baseball

American Baseball League
350 Park Avenue
18th Floor
New York, NY 10022

National Baseball League
350 Park Avenue
18th Floor
New York, NY 10022

Senior Professional Baseball Association
1000 Ponce de Leon Blvd.
Suite 201
Coral Gables, FL 33134

Basketball

Continental Basketball Association
425 South Cherry Street
Suite 230
Denver, CO 80222

National Basketball Association
Olympic Tower
645 Fifth Avenue
New York, NY 10022

Football

Canadian Football League
1200 Bay Street
12th Floor
Toronto, Ontario
Canada M5R 2A5

National Football League
410 Park Avenue
New York, NY 10022

Hockey

National Hockey League
650 Fifth Avenue
33rd Floor
New York, NY 10019

Q: LEAGUE OFFICE ADDRESSES (continued)

Soccer

American Football Association
135 Prospect
Elmhurst, IL 60126

Canadian Soccer League
5310 Explorer Drive
Mississauga, Ontario
Canada L4W 4J6

Mid-Atlantic Football Conference
4448 Strahle Street
Philadelphia, PA 19136

Western Soccer League
2815 Second Avenue
Suite 590
Seattle, WA 98121

R: HALL OF FAME ADDRESSES

Baseball Hall of Fame
Cooperstown, NY 13326

Naismith Memorial
Basketball Hall of Fame
P.O. Box 179
1150 West Columbia Avenue
Springfield, MA 01101-0179

Pro Football Hall of Fame
2121 George Halas Drive N.W.
Canton, OH 44708

U.S. Hockey Hall of Fame
U.S. Highway 53
Eveleth, MN 55734

S: INTERNATIONAL SPORTS ADDRESSES

Baseball

Japanese Baseball
Imperial Tower, 7F
1-1-1 Uchisaiwai-cho
Chiyoda-Ku
Tokyo 100
Japan

Mexican League
Angel Pola #16
Col. Periodista, C.P. 11220
Mexico, D.F.

Winter Baseball

Caribbean Baseball Confederation
171-A, C.P. 83190
Hermosillo, Sonora
Mexico

Dominican League
Av. De Febrero No. 218
Edificio Standard Quimica, 4ta Planta
Apartado Postal 1246
Santo Domingo, Dominican Republic

Mexican Pacific League
Pesqueria No. 401-R Altos
Edificio Borques
Navojoa, Sonora
Mexico

Puerto Rican League
Edificio First Federal
Ave. Munoz Rivera
Rio Piedras, PR 00928

Venezuelan League
Avenida Sorbona
Edif. Marta-2do. Piso
No. 25, Colinas de Bello Monte
Caracas, Venezuela

Basketball

Puerto Rico Basketball Federation
GPO Box 3947
San Juan, PR 00936

S: INTERNATIONAL SPORTS ADDRESSES (continued)

Note: Worldwide there are professional basketball federations established in 177 countries. However, contacting these, let alone locating individual teams, can be difficult. Professional basketball located outside the United States and Canada is relatively new, and the individual teams as well as each country's professional playing association often lack the organization and staying power we are accustomed to with the NBA. Over the coming years this is sure to change; however, for now here are two addresses that may be helpful resources for *specific* questions only.

FIBA (International Basketball Federation)
P.O. Box 700607
8000 Munick 70
Germany

USA Basketball Federation (Branch of the
    international federation)
1750 East Boulder Street
Colorado Springs, CO 80909

Football

African Football Confederation
5 Gabalaya Street
Gezira
Cairo, Egypt

Asian Football Confederation
93 E Jalan Maharajalela
Kuala Lumpur 50150
Malaysia

International Federation of Association
    Football
Hitzigweg 11
Postfach 85
8030 Zurich
Switzerland

Union of Arab Football Association
Olympic Complex
Deriyyah Road
P.O. Box 6040
Riyadh 11442
Saudi Arabia

T: PROFESSIONAL GOLF AND TENNIS ADDRESSES

Professional Golf Association of America
(PGA)
P.O. Box 109601
100 Avenue of the Champions
Palm Beach Gardens, FL 33410-9601

Ladies' Professional Golf Association (LPGA)
2570 Volusia Avenue
Daytona Beach, FL 32014

Men's Pro Tennis Council
437 Madison Avenue
New York, NY 10022

U.S. Tennis Association
1212 Avenue of the Americas, 12th Floor
New York, NY 10036

U: COLLEGE ADDRESSES

Here is a partial list of colleges and universities with popular athletic programs.

Arizona State University
Tempe, AZ 85287

Canadian Interuniversity
Athletic Union
1600 James Naismith Drive
Gloucester, Ontario
Canada K1B 5N4

Duke University
Durham, NC 27706

Florida State University
Tallahassee, FL 32306

Georgetown University
Washington, DC 20057

Indiana State University
Terre Haute, IN 47809

Indiana University
Bloomington, IN 47405

Michigan State University
East Lansing, MI 48824-1046

Ohio State University
Columbus, OH 43210-1358

Oklahoma University
660 Parrington Oval
Norman, OK 73019

Purdue University
West Lafayette, IN 47907

Stanford University
Stanford, CA 94305-1684

Texas A&M
College Station, TX 77843-1246

United States Air Force Academy
USAF Academy, CO 80840-5651

United States Coast Guard Academy
New London, CT 06320-4195

U: COLLEGE ADDRESSES (continued)

United States Naval Academy
Annapolis, MD 21402

University of Arizona
Tucson, AZ 85721

University of Arkansas
33rd and University
Little Rock, AR 72204

University of California — Berkeley
Berkeley, CA 94720

University of Georgia
Athens, GA 30602

University of Kansas
Lawrence, KS 66045

University of Kentucky
Lexington, KY 40506

University of Miami
University Station
Coral Gables, FL 33124

University of Michigan
1000 South Street
Ann Arbor, MI 48109

University of Nevada — Las Vegas
4505 South Maryland Parkway
Las Vegas, NV 89154

University of Southern California
University Park
Los Angeles, CA 90089-0012

Conferences

Atlantic Coast Conference
P.O. Drawer ACC
Greensboro, NC 27419-6999

Big Eight
104 West 9th Street
Suite 408
Kansas City, MO 64105

U: COLLEGE ADDRESSES (continued)

Big Sky
P.O. Box 1736
Boise, ID 83701

Big Ten
1111 Plaza Drive
Suite 600
Schaumburg, IL 60173

Big West
1700 East Dyer Road
Suite 140
Santa Ana, CA 92705

Colonial League
3897 Adler Place
Suite 310
Bethlehem, PA 18017

Gateway Conference
7700 Clayton Road
Suite 107
St. Louis, MO 63117

Ivy League
70 Washington Road
Princeton, NJ 08540

Mid-American
4 Sea Gate
Suite 102
Toledo, OH 43604

NAIA
1221 Baltimore Street
Kansas City, MO 64105

NCAA
P.O. Box 1906
Shawnee, KS 66201

NJCAA
P.O. Box 7305
Colorado Springs, CO 80933

Ohio Valley Conference
278 Franklin Road
Suite 103
Brentwood, TN 37027

U: COLLEGE ADDRESSES
(continued)

Pacific 10
800 South Broadway
Suite 400
Walnut Creek, CA 94596

Southland Conference
1309 West 15th Street
Suite 303
Plano, TX 75075

Western Athletic Conference
14 West Dry Creek Circle
Littleton, CO 80120

Yankee Conference
SID Office
University of New Hampshire
Durham, NH 03824

V: ITEMS PEOPLE COLLECT

The following is a partial list of items that people collect, which can be used for your general information.

Autographs
Balls
Banners
Bats
Buttons
Card Wrappers
Cards
Coins
Decals
Game Programs
Hats
Key Chains
Newspapers
Photographs
Posters
Press Pins
Schedules
Scorecards
Sports Books
Sports Publications
Stamps (domestic and foreign)
Ticket Stubs
Uniforms
Any items with the team logo (clothing, mugs, lamps, trash cans, clocks, etc.)

W: SPORTS PUBLICATIONS

With the increasing popularity of sports and sports collectibles, certain periodicals have been developed to keep the interested informed. These periodicals often feature articles that highlight available memorabilia, as well as feature classified ads. The following is a partial list of sports- and collectible-related publications.

Allan Kaye's Football Cards
The Baseball Address List
Baseball Card News
Baseball Card Price Guide
Baseball Cards
Baseball Digest
Baseball Update and Market Report
Basketball Digest
Beckett Baseball Card Monthly
Beckett Basketball Magazine
Beckett Football Magazine
Beckett Hockey Magazine
Football Card News and Price Guide
Football Card Price Guide
Football Digest
Game Player's Sports for Kids
Hockey Digest
Paper Collectors Marketplace
The Sporting News
Sports Card Trader
Sports Collectors Digest
Sports Illustrated for Kids
Standard Catalog of Baseball Cards
Topps Magazine
The Trader Speaks

X: COMPANY ADDRESSES

Borden Inc.
(Cracker Jack)
277 Park Avenue
New York, NY 10172

Coca-Cola
310 North Avenue
Atlanta, GA 30313

Dean Foods
(Baskin-Robbins)
3600 North River Road
Franklin Park, IL 60131

Eastman Kodak
343 State Street
Rochester, NY 14650

General Mills (cereals)
P.O. Box 1113
Minneapolis, MN 55440

Kellogg Co. (cereals)
Battle Creek, MI 49016

K-MART
3100 West Big Beaver Road
Troy, MI 48084

National Pizza
(Pizza Hut)
720 West 20th Street
Pittsburg, KS 66762

Here are a few of the many publications available as research guides.

X: COMPANY ADDRESSES
(continued)

PepsiCo, Inc.
World Headquarters
Purchase, NY 10577

Phillip Morris
(Kraft, Kool-aid, Post cereals)
120 Park Avenue
New York, NY 10017

Quaker Oats
Quaker Tower
P.O. Box 9001
Chicago, IL 60604

Ralston Purina
(cereals, Hostess)
Checkerboard Square
St. Louis, MO 63164

Toys 'R Us
461 From Road
Paramus, NJ 07652

Wendy's International
4288 West Dublin-Granville Road
Dublin, OH 43017

Wrigley
410 North Michigan Avenue
Chicago, IL 60611

Y: CARD MANUFACTURER ADDRESSES

Donruss Company
975 Kansas Street
Memphis, TN 38106

Fleer Corporation
10th and Somerville
Philadelphia, PA 19141

Jogo Inc.
1872 Queensdale Avenue
Gloucester, Ontario
Canada K1T 1K1

NBA HOOPS
P.O. Box 731
Durham, NC 27702

Score & Sportflics
25 Ford Road
Westport, CT 06880

Topps Gum Company
254 36th Street
Brooklyn, NY 11232

Upper Deck Company
1174 North Grove Street
Anaheim, CA 92806

Collectors Marketing Corporation
220 12th Avenue
New York, NY 10001

Pro Set Inc.
15303 Dallas Parkway #336
Dallas, TX 75248

ProCards
202 South Hanover Street
Pottstown, PA 19464

Swell
Philadelphia Chewing Gum Corporation
Havertown, PA 19083-2198

Z: SAMPLE INVENTORY SHEET

Control #	Description	Cost	Date Acquired	Condition	Current Est. Value
	INVENTORY SHEET PAGE 2 OF 2				
027	Boston Celtics Bumper Sticker	FREE	1/90	MINT	1⁵⁰
028	Ken Griffey, Jr. 1990 Team Schedule	FREE	5/90	MINT	1⁵⁰
029	Baltimore Orioles Round 2¼" Decal	FREE	5/90	MINT	50¢
030	4 Misc. 1990-91 Phila. Eagles Pro-Set Football Cards	FREE	10/90	MINT	1⁰⁰
031	1971 Topps O.J. Simpson Football Card	TRADE SEE NOTE	1/91	EXCELLENT NEARMINT	45⁰⁰
	NOTE: Traded for 1971 Topps Tarkenton/Butkus & 2 1967 Football Commons				
032	Matt Williams San Francisco Giants Postcard	FREE	4/91	MINT	1⁰⁰

Part IV
Collection Inventory

INVENTORY SHEET   PAGE _____ OF_____

Control #	Description	Cost	Date Acquired	Condition	Current Est. Value

INVENTORY SHEET		PAGE _____ OF _____			
Control #	Description	Cost	Date Acquired	Condition	Current Est. Value

INVENTORY SHEET		PAGE _____ OF_____			
Control #	Description	Cost	Date Acquired	Condition	Current Est. Value

INVENTORY SHEET			PAGE _____ OF_____		
Control #	**Description**	**Cost**	**Date Acquired**	**Condition**	**Current Est. Value**

INVENTORY SHEET   PAGE _____ OF_____

Control #	Description	Cost	Date Acquired	Condition	Current Est. Value

INVENTORY SHEET   PAGE _____ OF _____

Control #	Description	Cost	Date Acquired	Condition	Current Est. Value

INVENTORY SHEET　　　　PAGE _____ OF _____

Control #	Description	Cost	Date Acquired	Condition	Current Est. Value

INVENTORY SHEET   PAGE _____ OF _____

Control #	Description	Cost	Date Acquired	Condition	Current Est. Value

INVENTORY SHEET

PAGE _____ OF _____

Control #	Description	Cost	Date Acquired	Condition	Current Est. Value

INVENTORY SHEET   PAGE _____ OF _____

Control #	Description	Cost	Date Acquired	Condition	Current Est. Value

INVENTORY SHEET		PAGE _____ OF _____				
Control #	Description		Cost	Date Acquired	Condition	Current Est. Value

INVENTORY SHEET   PAGE _____ OF_____

Control #	Description	Cost	Date Acquired	Condition	Current Est. Value

INVENTORY SHEET

PAGE _____ OF_____

Control #	Description	Cost	Date Acquired	Condition	Current Est. Value

INVENTORY SHEET   PAGE _____ OF_____

Control #	Description	Cost	Date Acquired	Condition	Current Est. Value

Index